TRAVEL JUMBLE®

PUZZLES ON THE MOVE!

TRIUMPH®
BOOKS

This book is available at special discounts
for your group or organization.

For further information, contact:

Triumph Books LLC
814 North Franklin Street
Chicago, IL 60610
(800) 888-4741
(312) 337-1807 FAX

ISBN 1-57243-198-9

Printed in the USA

ISBN 978-1-57243-198-0

CONTENTS

- · - · ·· - ·· - · - · ·· -

CLASSIC

- · - ·· - · - ·· - · -

DAILY

- · - ·· - · - ·· - · -

CHALLENGER

- · - ·· - · - ·· - · -

ANSWERS

CLASSIC

TRAVEL JUMBLE®

JUMBLE®

Unscramble these four Jumbles, one letter to each square, to form four ordinary words.

BIATH

LUFTO

URAUBE

MAMBEL

THIS MIGHT BE *THERE* IN OUTER SPACE!

Now arrange the circled letters to form the surprise answer, as suggested by the above cartoon.

Print the SURPRISE ANSWER here

JUMBLE®

Unscramble these four Jumbles, one letter to each square, to form four ordinary words.

ATLAN

OONNI

FLYJOU

MASTIG

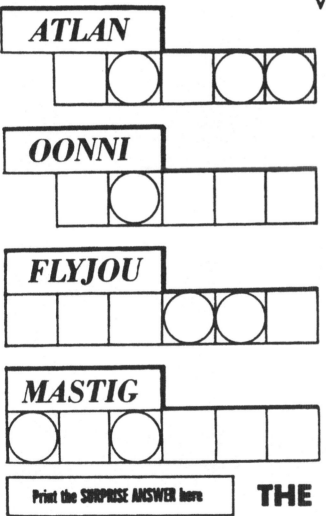

Virus?

HOW AN ORIENTAL GOT TO HEAVEN.

Now arrange the circled letters to form the surprise answer, as suggested by the above cartoon.

Print the SURPRISE ANSWER here

THE

JUMBLE®

Unscramble these four Jumbles, one letter to each square, to form four ordinary words.

ZENOO

VALIT

MEEPID

COYPIL

But WHY must you go?

Ugh!

A MOTIVE FOR A JOURNEY.

Now arrange the circled letters to form the surprise answer, as suggested by the above cartoon.

Print the SURPRISE ANSWER here A ◯◯◯◯◯ – ◯◯◯◯◯◯◯

JUMBLE®

Unscramble these four Jumbles,
one letter to each square, to
form four ordinary words.

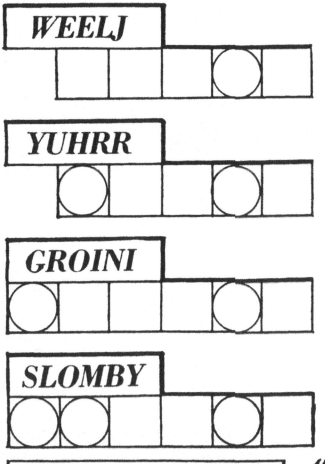

WEELJ

YUHRR

GROINI

SLOMBY

Print the SURPRISE ANSWER here

Back home in . . .

A COVER-UP IN
INDIANA.

Now arrange the circled letters
to form the surprise answer, as
suggested by the above cartoon.

" ◯◯◯◯◯◯◯◯ "

JUMBLE®

Unscramble these four Jumbles,
one letter to each square, to
form four ordinary words.

SNAIE

WARLD

CELTIN

MECION

Print the SURPRISE ANSWER here

WHAT SKYWRITERS WRITE.

Now arrange the circled letters
to form the surprise answer, as
suggested by the above cartoon.

JUMBLE®

Unscramble these four Jumbles, one letter to each square, to form four ordinary words.

SUYFS

TOROB

VOUDER

RENITE

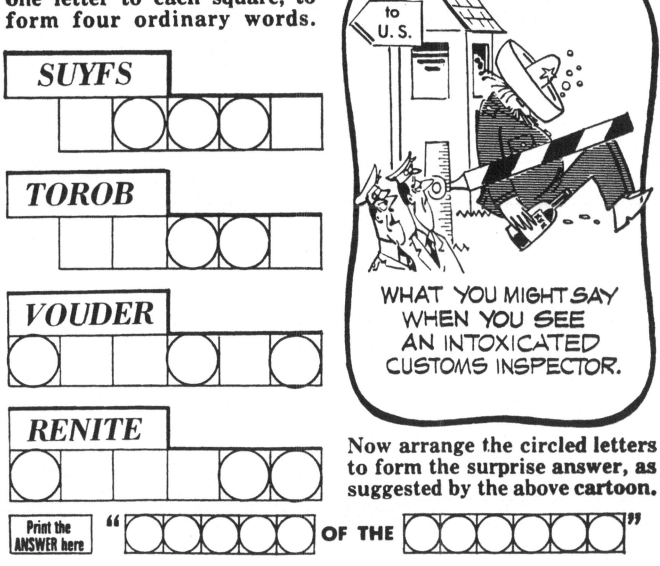

WHAT YOU MIGHT SAY WHEN YOU SEE AN INTOXICATED CUSTOMS INSPECTOR.

Now arrange the circled letters to form the surprise answer, as suggested by the above cartoon.

Print the ANSWER here " ◯◯◯◯◯ " OF THE " ◯◯◯◯◯◯ "

JUMBLE®

Unscramble these four Jumbles,
one letter to each square, to
form four ordinary words.

IRFEY

NAPAG

BOILEM

RIMPIA

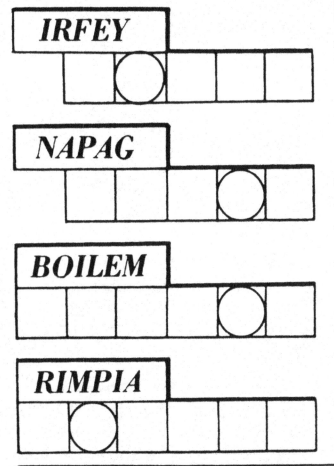

RAL STORE

POST OFFICE

WHERE YOU
MIGHT GET MAIL
IN OHIO.

Now arrange the circled letters
to form the surprise answer, as
suggested by the above cartoon.

Print the SURPRISE ANSWER here

FROM ◯◯◯◯

JUMBLE®

Unscramble these four Jumbles,
one letter to each square, to
form four ordinary words.

ILEEX

MARFE

ANIZIN

TALFOA

WHAT A MOROCCAN
SAID TO SOMEONE
HE HADN'T SEEN
IN YEARS.

Now arrange the circled letters
to form the surprise answer, as
suggested by the above cartoon.

 ANSWER here **YOUR**  **IS**

JUMBLE®

Unscramble these four Jumbles, one letter to each square, to form four ordinary words.

RUPUS

GEREM

BABFLY

STEJER

This is where it's at

CURRENTLY INFLUENTIAL AROUND THE SOUTH-EASTERN U.S. COAST.

Now arrange the circled letters to form the surprise answer, as suggested by the above cartoon.

Print the SURPRISE ANSWER here

THE

JUMBLE®

Unscramble these four Jumbles,
one letter to each square, to
form four ordinary words.

GUNST

NOYGA

REHNID

WEEYAL

Alabama
Alaska
Arizona

WHAT TO SAY WHEN
ASKED TO NAME THE
CAPITAL OF ALL
THE STATES.

Now arrange the circled letters
to form the surprise answer, as
suggested by the above cartoon.

Print the SURPRISE ANSWER here

" ◯◯◯◯◯◯◯◯◯◯◯ "

JUMBLE®

Unscramble these four Jumbles, one letter to each square, to form four ordinary words.

TRYAR

KORPE

TEABED

GREATY

Print the SURPRISE ANSWER here

This'll cost me a tip

GAS

OFTEN CHARGED FOR BETTER SERVICE.

Now arrange the circled letters to form the surprise answer, as suggested by the above cartoon.

A

JUMBLE®

Unscramble these four Jumbles, one letter to each square, to form four ordinary words.

PHULS

NOIBS

VIQUER

TIVEHR

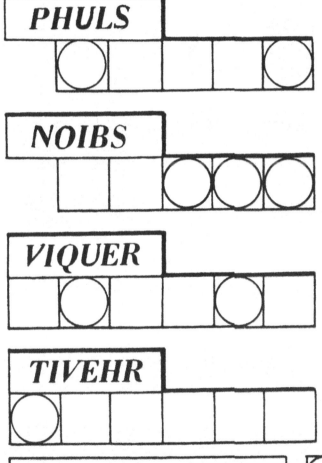

Did you think you could get away with THAT?

WHAT THE CUSTOMS INSPECTOR SAID THE SMUGGLER'S CASE WAS.

Now arrange the circled letters to form the surprise answer, as suggested by the above cartoon.

Print the SURPRISE ANSWER here

JUMBLE®

Unscramble these four Jumbles, one letter to each square, to form four ordinary words.

ROGAC

MYPTE

UNEAVE

SYMICT

How much did you say?

I'll introduce you

WHAT THEY SAID ABOUT THE PRETTY LADY CABDRIVER.

Now arrange the circled letters to form the surprise answer, as suggested by the above cartoon.

Print the SURPRISE ANSWER here

YOU "◯◯◯◯◯ ◯◯◯◯◯"

JUMBLE®

Unscramble these four Jumbles, one letter to each square, to form four ordinary words.

DOLMY

BIADE

URGETT

SVALIE

WHAT THEY SAID TO THE GUY WHO WAS TAKING A TRIP ON A TRAMP STEAMER.

Now arrange the circled letters to form the surprise answer, as suggested by the above cartoon.

Print the SURPRISE ANSWER here

" ⬡⬡⬡ ⬡⬡⬡⬡⬡⬡ "

JUMBLE®

Unscramble these four Jumbles,
one letter to each square, to
form four ordinary words.

PLUIP

VERAB

WORMAR

VICADE

KEEP AMERICA BEAUTIFUL

THIS MIGHT GROW IN A JUNKYARD.

Now arrange the circled letters
to form the surprise answer, as
suggested by the above cartoon.

Print the SURPRISE ANSWER here A ◯◯◯◯◯◯ ◯◯◯◯

JUMBLE®

Unscramble these four Jumbles,
one letter to each square, to
form four ordinary words.

NISEG

DAUGY

SHRUPE

YAUBET

Ulp!

Boy—am I
saving money!

SMALL CARS
RELIEVE THIS.

Now arrange the circled letters
to form the surprise answer, as
suggested by the above cartoon.

Print the SURPRISE ANSWER here

" ' "

JUMBLE®

Unscramble these four Jumbles,
one letter to each square, to
form four ordinary words.

OPTIV

MOURF

TANDLE

AMIDDY

Hi, baby!

RESTAURA

Menu:
STEAK DINNER ...$
CHICKEN " ...$
LAMB " ...$

Fresh!

IT'S THE SAME IN
MANY COUNTRIES.

Now arrange the circled letters
to form the surprise answer, as
suggested by the above cartoon.

Print the SURPRISE ANSWER here

" ◯◯◯◯◯ "

JUMBLE®

Unscramble these four Jumbles,
one letter to each square, to
form four ordinary words.

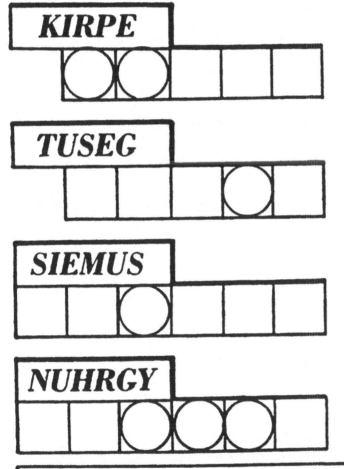

KIRPE

TUSEG

SIEMUS

NUHRGY

Print the SURPRISE ANSWER here

CAR RENTAL AGENCY

THEY CONTRACT TO
GIVE YOU A
COMFORTABLE RIDE.

Now arrange the circled letters
to form the surprise answer, as
suggested by the above cartoon.

JUMBLE®

Unscramble these four Jumbles, one letter to each square, to form four ordinary words.

OCCIL

KYKIN

DAUSIN

QUAPEL

Now arrange the circled letters to form the surprise answer, as suggested by the above cartoon.

Print the SURPRISE ANSWER here

JUMBLE®

Unscramble these four Jumbles, one letter to each square, to form four ordinary words.

SEGUS

YEMSS

MEUGLE

RAPPOL

| Print the SURPRISE ANSWER here |

Let him go. He's clean.

HE DECLARED— HE WASN'T ONE !

Now arrange the circled letters to form the surprise answer, as suggested by the above cartoon.

A

JUMBLE®

Unscramble these four Jumbles,
one letter to each square, to
form four ordinary words.

MERIN

CRAFS

DORWYB

PENMAD

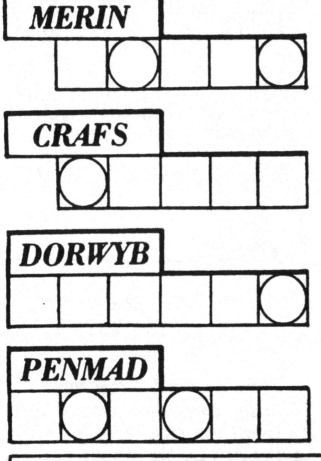

MAY BE SHOT
IN A BOAT.

Now arrange the circled letters
to form the surprise answer, as
suggested by the above cartoon.

Print the SURPRISE ANSWER here

JUMBLE®

Unscramble these four Jumbles,
one letter to each square, to
form four ordinary words.

TREHB

PINYP

INMALY

CLUMON

MEN IN PORT
ARE CONSPICUOUS.

Now arrange the circled letters
to form the surprise answer, as
suggested by the above cartoon. ..

Print the SURPRISE ANSWER here " "

JUMBLE®

Unscramble these four Jumbles,
one letter to each square, to
form four ordinary words.

HINEW

KARCC

UNDASE

REESHA

HOW TO CUT UP
IN A CAB.

Now arrange the circled letters
to form the surprise answer, as
suggested by the above cartoon.

Print the SURPRISE ANSWER here

A

JUMBLE®

Unscramble these four Jumbles,
one letter to each square, to
form four ordinary words.

NIORB

PUTIL

WODASH

YOGAVE

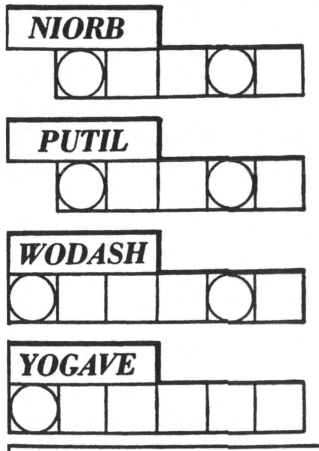

So nice of you to come

YOU WOULDN'T EXPECT
TO FIND HER
AT HOME!

Now arrange the circled letters
to form the surprise answer, as
suggested by the above cartoon.

Print the SURPRISE ANSWER here

A

JUMBLE®

Unscramble these four Jumbles, one letter to each square, to form four ordinary words.

ROODE

MOBZI

RENOSP

HAWRTT

A TRAVELER HAS ABSOLUTELY NO CHANCE OF GETTING ON THIS LINE!

Now arrange the circled letters to form the surprise answer, as suggested by the above cartoon.

Print the SURPRISE ANSWER here

THE ◯◯◯◯◯◯◯

DAILY

TRAVEL
JUMBLE®

JUMBLE®

Unscramble these four Jumbles, one letter to each square, to form four ordinary words.

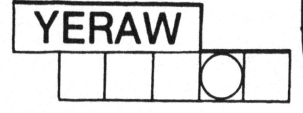

YERAW

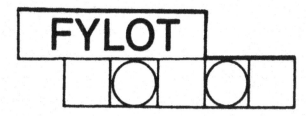

FYLOT

ERVEWS

NIRBON

London tomorrow ... next, Paris ... then back to the Met

FOR THESE OPERA SINGERS—COULD BE NO REST.

Now arrange the circled letters to form the surprise answer, as suggested by the above cartoon.

Print answer here:

JUMBLE®

Unscramble these four Jumbles,
one letter to each square, to form
four ordinary words.

BROEP

TABEA

PHANEP

SINIST

COULD BE THE
REASON—FOR HAVING
MARRIED IN SPAIN.

Now arrange the circled letters to
form the surprise answer, as suggested by the above cartoon.

Answer here: "⬭⬭⬭ ⬭⬭⬭⬭⬭⬭"

JUMBLE®

Unscramble these four Jumbles, one letter to each square, to form four ordinary words.

WONGI

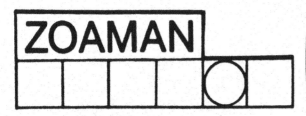

YERME

ZOAMAN

DROBIF

Don't look!

WHAT YOU MIGHT FIND IN BORNEO— ON A NATIVE.

Now arrange the circled letters to form the surprise answer, as suggested by the above cartoon.

Print answer here: " ⬡⬡ ⬡⬡⬡⬡ "

JUMBLE®

Unscramble these four Jumbles, one letter to each square, to form four ordinary words.

MIDUH

ELVOG

ICETOX

GOPINE

WHAT "TEQUILA" IS.

Now arrange the circled letters to form the surprise answer, as suggested by the above cartoon.

Answer: THE "◯◯◯◯◯" OF ◯◯◯◯◯◯

31

JUMBLE®

Unscramble these four Jumbles,
one letter to each square, to form
four ordinary words.

YASTT

TULFE

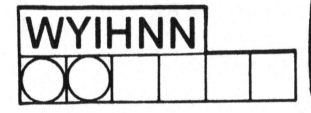

WYIHNN

GROINI

It's a flood!

THE TRAIN CARRYING
THE LAUNDRYMEN TO
WORK WAS DELAYED
BECAUSE OF THIS.

Now arrange the circled letters to
form the surprise answer, as suggested by the above cartoon.

Answer: "⬡⬡⬡⬡⬡ ⬡⬡⬡⬡" ON THE ⬡⬡⬡⬡

JUMBLE®

Unscramble these four Jumbles,
one letter to each square, to form
four ordinary words.

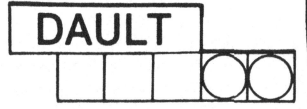

DAULT

ENNIL

CHOPON

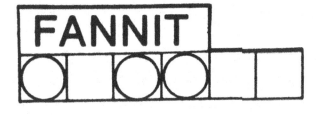

FANNIT

I suppose
he expects a
big tip

WHAT YOU HAVE TO
TAKE INTO CONSIDER-
ATION THESE DAYS
WHEN YOU HAVE YOUR
TIRES PUMPED UP.

Now arrange the circled letters to
form the surprise answer, as suggested by the above cartoon.

Print answer here:

JUMBLE.

Unscramble these four Jumbles,
one letter to each square, to form
four ordinary words.

ALYMN

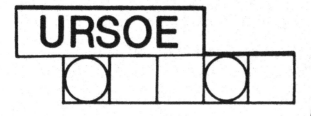

URSOE

NATTEX

TIPEOA

Stop! Lemme off!

WHAT MIXING UP
TRAINS MIGHT BE
FOR A TRAVELER.

Now arrange the circled letters to
form the surprise answer, as suggested by the above cartoon.

Print answer here: A "  "

JUMBLE®

Unscramble these four Jumbles, one letter to each square, to form four ordinary words.

EAPEY

GLOIN

LEHTAH

TREEMP

So this traveling salesman . . .

WHAT STORIES HEARD DURING A FLIGHT ARE EXPECTED TO BE.

Now arrange the circled letters to form the surprise answer, as suggested by the above cartoon.

Answer here: ON A

JUMBLE.

Unscramble these four Jumbles,
one letter to each square, to form
four ordinary words.

LOVEH

YURST

CHALUN

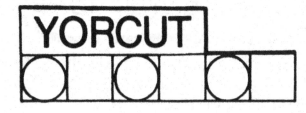

YORCUT

Quick! To the airport!

THE KING DECIDED
TO ABDICATE
RATHER THAN RISK
BEING THIS.

Now arrange the circled letters to
form the surprise answer, as suggested by the above cartoon.

Answer here: "  "

JUMBLE.

Unscramble these four Jumbles,
one letter to each square, to form
four ordinary words.

SOOGE

YILIC

HETOLC

DRAILZ

WHAT YOU HAVE
TO HAVE TO
SPOT A GLACIER.

Now arrange the circled letters to
form the surprise answer, as suggested by the above cartoon.

Answer here: GOOD

JUMBLE®

Unscramble these four Jumbles,
one letter to each square, to form
four ordinary words.

PLYAP

WAHSS

REFOBE

VINNET

WHEE-E

SCREECH!

SPOTS FROM
THE REAR.

Now arrange the circled letters to
form the surprise answer, as suggested by the above cartoon.

Print answer here: " ◯◯◯◯◯ "

JUMBLE.

Unscramble these four Jumbles, one letter to each square, to form four ordinary words.

OYLED

HASAW

NITIVE

HAPNOR

OUR ASTRONAUTS WILL LAND ON MARS WHEN THEY DO THIS.

PROGRAM OF ACTION

Now arrange the circled letters to form the surprise answer, as suggested by the above cartoon.

 Answer: " ☐☐☐☐☐☐ " THAT  ☐☐☐

JUMBLE.®

Unscramble these four Jumbles,
one letter to each square, to form
four ordinary words.

TUSEA

HOPOW

EMTYSS

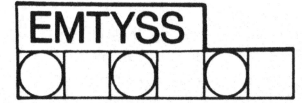
DEWPOR

Says he's going to the
North Pole when he
grows up

WHY A BAREFOOT
KID MIGHT REMIND
YOU OF AN ARCTIC
EXPLORER.

Now arrange the circled letters to
form the surprise answer, as suggested by the above cartoon.

Answer: HE ⬡⬡⬡⬡⬡ NO ⬡⬡⬡⬡⬡

JUMBLE.

Unscramble these four Jumbles, one letter to each square, to form four ordinary words.

MELIP

ALVAN

ANIZIN

SMURTI

ROOMS

Yuch!

WHAT THE MUSICIANS SAID THAT AWFUL HOTEL WAS.

Now arrange the circled letters to form the surprise answer, as suggested by the above cartoon.

Print answer here: A "   "

JUMBLE.

Unscramble these four Jumbles,
one letter to each square, to form
four ordinary words.

VINGY

ISSAB

DIPSUT

GININN

WHAT YOU USUALLY
PAY WHEN YOU
CALL ON SOMEONE.

Now arrange the circled letters to
form the surprise answer, as suggested by the above cartoon.

Print answer here:

JUMBLE®

Unscramble these four Jumbles,
one letter to each square, to form
four ordinary words.

ROMUN

GEEBI

YEMBOR

BRAYNE

ONE SIDE OF THE
STREET USUALLY
SHOWS IT EVEN.

Now arrange the circled letters to
form the surprise answer, as suggested by the above cartoon.

Print answer here:

JUMBLE.

Unscramble these four Jumbles,
one letter to each square, to form
four ordinary words.

KEHRI

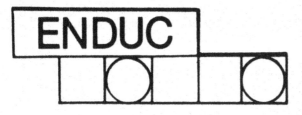

ENDUC

TRACCI

NODARP

IN WHAT STATE ARE
MOST PEOPLE BORN?

Now arrange the circled letters to
form the surprise answer, as suggested by the above cartoon.

Print answer here: "   "

JUMBLE®

Unscramble these four Jumbles,
one letter to each square, to form
four ordinary words.

INFEG

RAWLD

ASOURE

EMBALC

MIGHT BE
COMBAT PILOTS
IN SPACE SUITS.

Now arrange the circled letters to
form the surprise answer, as suggested by the above cartoon.

Print answer here: "  "

45

JUMBLE.

Unscramble these four Jumbles, one letter to each square, to form four ordinary words.

YERNT

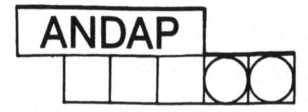

ANDAP

REVOUD

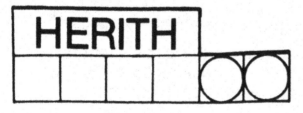

HERITH

THIS WILL HELP IF YOU'RE BADLY TIRED FOR DRIVING.

Now arrange the circled letters to form the surprise answer, as suggested by the above cartoon.

Print answer here: A

JUMBLE®

Unscramble these four Jumbles,
one letter to each square, to form
four ordinary words.

NEKIF

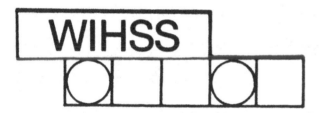

WIHSS

RAGUTI

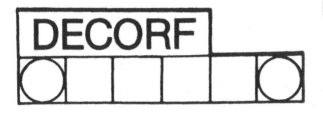

DECORF

This is no laughing matter!

WHAT ICE ON
THE ROAD IS.

Now arrange the circled letters to
form the surprise answer, as suggested by the above cartoon.

Print answer here:

JUMBLE.

Unscramble these four Jumbles, one letter to each square, to form four ordinary words.

HAWSS

SURBT

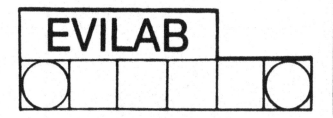

EVILAB

CLUPEO

WHAT A BEAUTY CONTEST JUDGE HAS TO KNOW HOW TO DO.

Now arrange the circled letters to form the surprise answer, as suggested by the above cartoon.

 Answer:  ON

JUMBLE.

Unscramble these four Jumbles,
one letter to each square, to form
four ordinary words.

LAVIT

CUMSI

TIENNY

CLIFEK

WHY HE INSISTED
ON WEARING
SEAT BELTS.

Now arrange the circled letters to
form the surprise answer, as suggested by the above cartoon.

Print answer here: TO  HIS

JUMBLE.

Unscramble these four Jumbles,
one letter to each square, to form
four ordinary words.

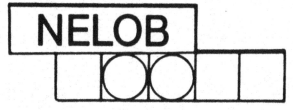

NELOB

HESAF

LEGGIG

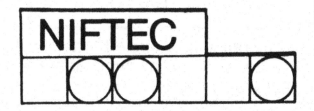

NIFTEC

WHAT THAT FRUS-
TRATED ASTRONAUT
WAS ALWAYS DOING
AT HOME.

Now arrange the circled letters to
form the surprise answer, as suggested by the above cartoon.

Answer:

JUMBLE®

Unscramble these four Jumbles,
one letter to each square, to form
four ordinary words.

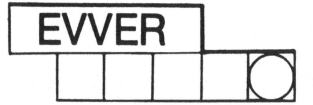

EVVER

LEBLE

GICART

YARWIA

WHAT THEY CALLED
THE MAN WHO PUT
GLASS INTO THE
IGLOO WINDOWS.

Now arrange the circled letters to
form the surprise answer, as suggested by the above cartoon.

Answer here: THE " ⬡⬡⬡⬡⬡⬡⬡ "

51

JUMBLE®

Unscramble these four Jumbles, one letter to each square, to form four ordinary words.

DANSY

NELLK

PURROA

GETULL

WHAT A BACKSEAT DRIVER NEVER SEEMS TO DO.

Now arrange the circled letters to form the surprise answer, as suggested by the above cartoon.

Answer here: ☐☐☐ OUT OF "☐☐☐"

JUMBLE®

Unscramble these four Jumbles,
one letter to each square, to form
four ordinary words.

HUBYS

RASCY

NAHDDE

RICOTE

Oops!

BEGINNER

WHAT HE APPARENTLY
TOOK IN ORDER TO
LEARN TO DRIVE.

Now arrange the circled letters to
form the surprise answer, as suggested by the above cartoon.

Answer: A "⬚⬚⬚⬚⬚" ⬚⬚⬚⬚⬚⬚

JUMBLE.

Unscramble these four Jumbles,
one letter to each square, to form
four ordinary words.

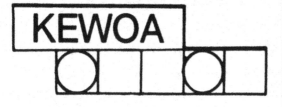

KEWOA

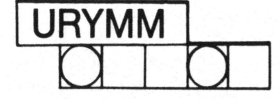

URYMM

SACCUT

CEPTIK

WHAT THE RAILROAD
MAN SAID TO THE
HOBO WHO WAS
TRYING TO STEAL
A RIDE.

Now arrange the circled letters to
form the surprise answer, as suggested by the above cartoon.

Answer: ⬡⬡⬡⬡ ⬡⬡⬡⬡⬡ !

JUMBLE.

Unscramble these four Jumbles,
one letter to each square, to form
four ordinary words.

THOOP

BASUQ

NAEVLE

MUGNIP

WHAT "HMS
PINAFORE" COULD
UNDOUBTEDLY BE.

Now arrange the circled letters to
form the surprise answer, as suggested by the above cartoon.

Answer here: " ⬡⬡⬡⬡ FOR ⬡⬡⬡⬡ "

JUMBLE®

Unscramble these four Jumbles, one letter to each square, to form four ordinary words.

AUPSE

MERFA

NEXETT

TROBEH

I've eaten in better places

WHAT WAS THE TROUBLE WITH THE RESTAURANT THEY OPENED UP ON THE MOON?

Now arrange the circled letters to form the surprise answer, as suggested by the above cartoon.

Answer: IT HAD "NO ◯◯◯◯◯◯◯◯◯◯◯"

JUMBLE.

Unscramble these four Jumbles,
one letter to each square, to form
four ordinary words.

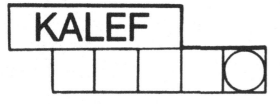

KALEF

GUAVE

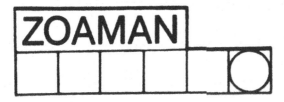

ZOAMAN

GEEREM

LIGHTLY GIVES YOU
THE GO-AHEAD.

Now arrange the circled letters to
form the surprise answer, as suggested by the above cartoon.

Print answer here:

JUMBLE®

Unscramble these four Jumbles,
one letter to each square, to form
four ordinary words.

EGBIE

YONPE

DUSSIC

GREFOT

WHAT A
MURKY FOG
GIVES DRIVERS.

Now arrange the circled letters to
form the surprise answer, as suggested by the above cartoon.

Print answer here: THE " ◯◯◯◯◯◯ "

JUMBLE.

Unscramble these four Jumbles,
one letter to each square, to form
four ordinary words.

TREXE

TCHEF

LAWTUN

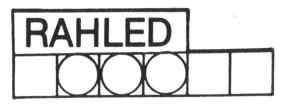

RAHLED

WHAT A
RAINY DAY IS
FOR A CABDRIVER.

Now arrange the circled letters to
form the surprise answer, as suggested by the above cartoon.

Answer: "⬡⬡⬡⬡" ⬡⬡⬡⬡⬡⬡⬡⬡

JUMBLE.

Unscramble these four Jumbles, one letter to each square, to form four ordinary words.

TYSOO

NOAKE

HARTER

MURTES

We've found them all!

WHAT YOU MIGHT GET FROM ASTRONOMERS.

Now arrange the circled letters to form the surprise answer, as suggested by the above cartoon.

Answer: " ⬡⬡⬡ ⬡⬡⬡⬡ ⬡⬡⬡⬡⬡ "

JUMBLE.

Unscramble these four Jumbles,
one letter to each square, to form
four ordinary words.

NAUHM

ARBSS

DECLUD

POATTE

It wasn't there yesterday

WHAT HE WAS
WHEN HE SAW
THAT TREE TRUNK
RIGHT IN THE
MIDDLE OF THE ROAD.

Now arrange the circled letters to
form the surprise answer, as suggested by the above cartoon.

Print answer here: "⬡⬡⬡⬡⬡⬡⬡"

JUMBLE.

Unscramble these four Jumbles, one letter to each square, to form four ordinary words.

KELLN

NYNIF

PRITOM

LENCAG

Lucky to find such a good place

THERE'S USUALLY A FINE FOR PARKING IN ANY SPOT THAT'S THIS.

Now arrange the circled letters to form the surprise answer, as suggested by the above cartoon.

Answer: ☐◯◯◯◯☐ FOR ◯◯◯◯◯◯◯◯

JUMBLE.

Unscramble these four Jumbles,
one letter to each square, to form
four ordinary words.

ATLAN

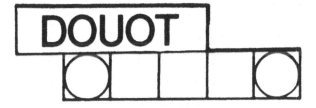

DOUOT

ENGOIP

CHUTOY

They must
all be
crazy

WHAT FORM OF
LOCOMOTION
IS DRAG RACING?

Now arrange the circled letters to
form the surprise answer, as suggested by the above cartoon.

Answer: A "⬭⬭⬭⬭" ⬭⬭⬭⬭⬭⬭

JUMBLE®

Unscramble these four Jumbles,
one letter to each square, to form
four ordinary words.

PEBID

BUMIE

EXTUDO

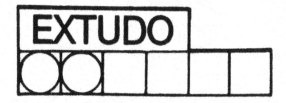

GAMNEA

Forget it

$75,000

WHAT TO
DO WHEN YOU
HAVE THE FEELING
YOU WANT TO
SPEND MORE THAN
YOU CAN AFFORD.

Now arrange the circled letters to
form the surprise answer, as suggested by the above cartoon.

Answer: ◯◯◯ IT IN " ◯◯◯ – ◯◯◯ "
THE

JUMBLE.

Unscramble these four Jumbles, one letter to each square, to form four ordinary words.

YOMSS

EUQUE

TAUMER

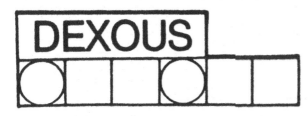

DEXOUS

AN IMPATIENT DRIVER WHO HAS TO STOP FOR A TRAFFIC LIGHT USUALLY DOES THIS.

11-12

Now arrange the circled letters to form the surprise answer, as suggested by the above cartoon.

Print answer here:

JUMBLE®

Unscramble these four Jumbles,
one letter to each square, to form
four ordinary words.

REBLY

PLYAP

LETLIF

BROIMD

I'm thirsty

THE BEST WINE
AFTER A
LONG VOYAGE.

Now arrange the circled letters to
form the surprise answer, as suggested by the above cartoon.

Print answer here:

JUMBLE.

Unscramble these four Jumbles, one letter to each square, to form four ordinary words.

TRAFE

MELIP

FUMINF

WENTIG

Hurray! No school!

He won't be in

WHAT A BLIZZARD MIGHT DO TO DAILY LIFE.

Now arrange the circled letters to form the surprise answer, as suggested by the above cartoon.

Answer: " ⬡⬡⬡⬡⬡⬡ – ⬡⬡⬡ " IT

JUMBLE.

Unscramble these four Jumbles,
one letter to each square, to form
four ordinary words.

TRUIF

DALLE

CADAFE

JERPUM

SPEED
LIMIT
50
MPH

THE ONLY TIME
SOME DRIVERS OBEY
THE SPEED LIMIT IS
WHEN THEY'RE THIS.

Now arrange the circled letters to
form the surprise answer, as suggested by the above cartoon.

Answer: IN A ☐☐☐☐☐☐☐ ☐☐☐

JUMBLE®

Unscramble these four Jumbles,
one letter to each square, to form
four ordinary words.

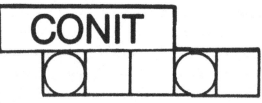

CONIT

SUBGO

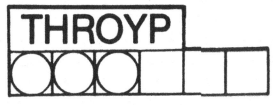

THROYP

DUMEGS

Whatever
happened
to trains?

Or
bikes?

Or
just
plain
walking?

WHAT MOST
VACATIONERS SEEM
TO BE THESE DAYS.

Now arrange the circled letters to
form the surprise answer, as suggested by the above cartoon.

Answer: "◯◯◯ - ◯◯◯◯◯ - ◯◯◯◯"

JUMBLE.

Unscramble these four Jumbles, one letter to each square, to form four ordinary words.

CABIS

FENTO

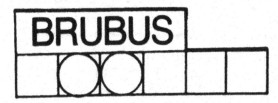
MEEDER

BRUBUS

Driven by a little old lady once a month

WHAT MANY A USED CAR IS NOT.

Now arrange the circled letters to form the surprise answer, as suggested by the above cartoon.

Answer here: WHAT IT

JUMBLE.

Unscramble these four Jumbles,
one letter to each square, to form
four ordinary words.

PRUTE

NUGOY

NERUNG

RAYTLE

A MAN SOLD ME THE NILE
RIVER FOR TEN DOLLARS

Now arrange the circled letters to
form the surprise answer, as suggested by the above cartoon.

Answer here: "  "

JUMBLE®

Unscramble these four Jumbles,
one letter to each square, to form
four ordinary words.

ILVIC

FLAIN

TERVID

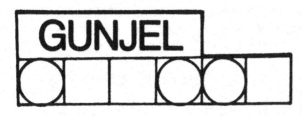

GUNJEL

HE WOULDN'T BE
IN SUCH A HURRY
IF HE KNEW HE
WAS THIS.

Now arrange the circled letters to
form the surprise answer, as suggested by the above cartoon.

Answer: ⬡⬡⬡⬡⬡⬡⬡ TO ⬡⬡⬡⬡

JUMBLE.

Unscramble these four Jumbles, one letter to each square, to form four ordinary words.

PALLE

LEREC

RORTER

TURBAP

WHAT THAT FIRST TAVERN IN THE ARCTIC WAS CALLED.

Now arrange the circled letters to form the surprise answer, as suggested by the above cartoon.

Print answer here: THE

73

JUMBLE.

Unscramble these four Jumbles, one letter to each square, to form four ordinary words.

NIFET

YANNO

DINGHI

TEXMEP

One degree above zero

So what? Who cares?

WHAT BITTER COLD WEATHER SOMETIMES IS.

Now arrange the circled letters to form the surprise answer, as suggested by the above cartoon.

Answer: ☐☐☐☐ TO "☐☐☐☐☐☐☐☐"

JUMBLE®

Unscramble these four Jumbles, one letter to each square, to form four ordinary words.

ANUFA

VAYEH

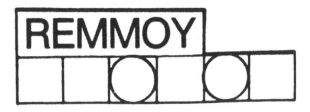

REMMOY

TAUMUN

Disgraceful

POLLUTION IS THE CONTAMINATION OF NATURE BY THIS.

Now arrange the circled letters to form the surprise answer, as suggested by the above cartoon.

Answer here:

JUMBLE.

Unscramble these four Jumbles, one letter to each square, to form four ordinary words.

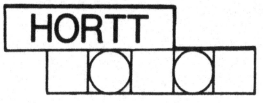

HORTT

YERNT

AJURAG

KRUBEE

Sad news?

WHAT THAT STORY ABOUT THE ONION CROP WAS.

Now arrange the circled letters to form the surprise answer, as suggested by the above cartoon.

Answer here: A

JUMBLE.

Unscramble these four Jumbles, one letter to each square, to form four ordinary words.

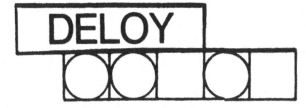

DELOY

NAPOC

TOZALE

PREJUM

THAT RECKLESS CHAUFFEUR MUST HAVE HAD A LICENSE TO DRIVE—

Now arrange the circled letters to form the surprise answer, as suggested by the above cartoon.

Answer:

JUMBLE®

Unscramble these four Jumbles,
one letter to each square, to form
four ordinary words.

ENATE

DARRO

TENCED

SPICHY

A DRIVER IS A
GUY WHO FORGETS
THAT HE USED
TO BE THIS.

Now arrange the circled letters to
form the surprise answer, as suggested by the above cartoon.

Answer here: A

78

JUMBLE.

Unscramble these four Jumbles, one letter to each square, to form four ordinary words.

YOGGS

CHAVO

GREATT

VISTEN

A PEDESTRIAN IS A PERSON WHO HAS LEARNED THAT IT DOESN'T ALWAYS PAY TO ---

Now arrange the circled letters to form the surprise answer, as suggested by the above cartoon.

Answer here:

JUMBLE.

Unscramble these four Jumbles,
one letter to each square, to form
four ordinary words.

LUMGO

VIPTO

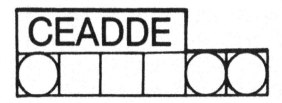

CEADDE

YALTER

IF YOU'RE LUCKY,
THAT USED CAR
WILL BE A PLEASURE
TO RIDE; IF NOT---

Now arrange the circled letters to
form the surprise answer, as suggested by the above cartoon.

Print answer here:

JUMBLE.

Unscramble these four Jumbles,
one letter to each square, to form
four ordinary words.

REBAG

LESIA

NORGAD

PELETS

WHAT A PERSON
WHO HAS FAILED TO
KEEP UP HIS PAY—
MENTS ON THE CAR
IS CALLED.

Now arrange the circled letters to
form the surprise answer, as suggested by the above cartoon.

Answer here: A

JUMBLE®

Unscramble these four Jumbles,
one letter to each square, to form
four ordinary words.

BOESE

RUSUY

SYMFIL

YUBILS

THE ONLY SURE
WAY OF CATCHING
THE NEXT TRAIN
IS TO ---

Now arrange the circled letters to
form the surprise answer, as suggested by the above cartoon.

Answer: ☐☐☐☐ THE ONE ☐☐☐☐☐☐☐

JUMBLE®

Unscramble these four Jumbles, one letter to each square, to form four ordinary words.

MOUDI

KANEL

BONGEY

GISTED

Weatherman was wrong again

HOW SPRING OFTEN COMES.

Now arrange the circled letters to form the surprise answer, as suggested by the above cartoon.

Print answer here: "  "

JUMBLE.

Unscramble these four Jumbles, one letter to each square, to form four ordinary words.

UNERP

DIEFT

KITSCY

SPEEXO

CUSTOMS

WHAT A SMUGGLER DOESN'T HAVE.

Now arrange the circled letters to form the surprise answer, as suggested by the above cartoon.

Answer here: A  OF

84

JUMBLE.

Unscramble these four Jumbles, one letter to each square, to form four ordinary words.

MOACE

ALAFT

INGARD

DOLBIE

You're grounded!

WHAT A PARENT'S MAJOR PROBLEM SOMETIMES IS.

Now arrange the circled letters to form the surprise answer, as suggested by the above cartoon.

Print answer here:

85

JUMBLE.

Unscramble these four Jumbles,
one letter to each square, to form
four ordinary words.

EDGUF

ALGIE

CLEBUK

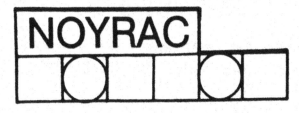

NOYRAC

WHATHAPPENSWHEN
AUTOMOBILESARESO
CLOSETOGETHERTHEY
CAN'TMOVE?

Now arrange the circled letters to
form the surprise answer, as suggested by the above cartoon.

Print answer here:

JUMBLE.

Unscramble these four Jumbles,
one letter to each square, to form
four ordinary words.

HESEP

ACTEX

WARROM

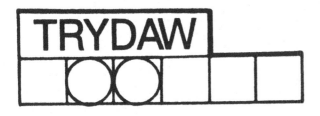
TRYDAW

Hey--where's my dough?

Haven't you
learned your
lesson yet?

IF YOU LEND A
PRETENDED "FRIEND"
MONEY, AND NEVER
SEE HIM AGAIN---

Now arrange the circled letters to
form the surprise answer, as suggested by the above cartoon.

Print answer here: IT  IT

JUMBLE®

Unscramble these four Jumbles,
one letter to each square, to form
four ordinary words.

RADUG

NARBD

MADORR

SAYNUE

THAT PIONEER
BLAZED A TRAIL
THROUGH THE
WILDERNESS, BUT NOW
HIS DESCENDANTS---

Now arrange the circled letters to
form the surprise answer, as suggested by the above cartoon.

Answer here: ⬡⬡⬡⬡ UP THE ⬡⬡⬡⬡

JUMBLE.

Unscramble these four Jumbles,
one letter to each square, to form
four ordinary words.

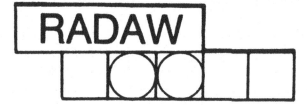

RADAW

MESOU

HELGGA

FRIEVY

THAT ROAD HOG
WAS WILLING TO
MEET ANY OTHER
DRIVER ----

Now arrange the circled letters to
form the surprise answer, as suggested by the above cartoon.

Answer: ⬡⬡⬡⬡ THAN ⬡⬡⬡⬡⬡⬡⬡

JUMBLE.

Unscramble these four Jumbles,
one letter to each square, to form
four ordinary words.

DEROO

TENGA

VIRLED

FULOWE

WHAT A
REVOLUTION MAKES.

Now arrange the circled letters to
form the surprise answer, as suggested by the above cartoon.

Answer: THE ⬡⬡⬡⬡⬡ GO ⬡⬡⬡⬡⬡

JUMBLE.

Unscramble these four Jumbles,
one letter to each square, to form
four ordinary words.

BRIHC

CINIG

LORCAR

THINGK

ALL THE CROOKS
IN THAT POLLUTED
CITY SEEM TO HAVE
VANISHED---

Now arrange the circled letters to
form the surprise answer, as suggested by the above cartoon.

Print answer here: INTO

JUMBLE®

Unscramble these four Jumbles,
one letter to each square, to form
four ordinary words.

GITHE

TILIM

HANVEE

DRAFIT

THE BEST WAY TO
STOP THE NOISE
IN THE BACK OF
YOUR CAR.

Now arrange the circled letters to
form the surprise answer, as suggested by the above cartoon.

Answer here:

JUMBLE.

Unscramble these four Jumbles,
one letter to each square, to form
four ordinary words.

IKKAH

LAUDT

YENTIJ

STICMY

WHEN A GROUP OF
FRIENDS BEGAN PLAY-
ING CARDS ON THE
PLANE, THEY
AGREED THAT---

Now arrange the circled letters to
form the surprise answer, as suggested by the above cartoon.

Answer here: THE ⬡⬡⬡ WAS THE ⬡⬡⬡⬡⬡⬡

JUMBLE.

Unscramble these four Jumbles,
one letter to each square, to form
four ordinary words.

DRATY

SNABI

BARNEY

REEMIP

MIGHT DESCRIBE
THE PLANET MARS.

Now arrange the circled letters to
form the surprise answer, as suggested by the above cartoon.

Answer: "⬚⬚⬚ --- ⬚⬚⬚⬚⬚⬚"

JUMBLE®

Unscramble these four Jumbles, one letter to each square, to form four ordinary words.

GRUPE

RABEG

REHNID

EXTORV

ASTRONOMY MIGHT BE THIS.

Now arrange the circled letters to form the surprise answer, as suggested by the above cartoon.

 Answer here: ◯◯◯◯ ONE'S ◯◯◯◯

JUMBLE.

Unscramble these four Jumbles,
one letter to each square, to form
four ordinary words.

TULIB

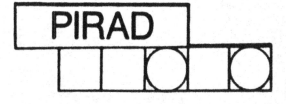

PIRAD

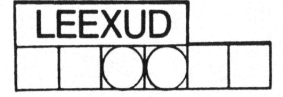

LEEXUD

MUPCIE

A PARATROOPER IS
JUST ABOUT THE ONLY
PERSON WHO CAN
CLIMB DOWN A TREE---

Now arrange the circled letters to
form the surprise answer, as suggested by the above cartoon.

Answer here: HE
NEVER

JUMBLE®

Unscramble these four Jumbles,
one letter to each square, to form
four ordinary words.

SACEE

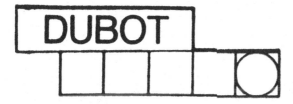

DUBOT

FACTRY

TIPSEC

WHEN HE STAYED
TOO LONG, THE
GUEST BECAME THIS.

Now arrange the circled letters to
form the surprise answer, as suggested by the above cartoon.

Print answer here:

JUMBLE.

Unscramble these four Jumbles,
one letter to each square, to form
four ordinary words.

NAIRY

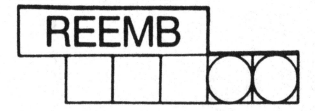

REEMB

CEERUD

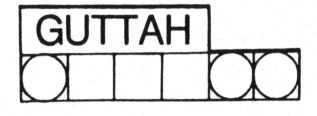

GUTTAH

SHE ALWAYS DRIVES
VERY SLOWLY BE-
CAUSE SHE WANTS TO
DO ANYTHING---

Now arrange the circled letters to
form the surprise answer, as suggested by the above cartoon.

Answer: TO STAY

JUMBLE®

Unscramble these four Jumbles,
one letter to each square, to form
four ordinary words.

ROWNC

LAWRB

DEGELP

THAILG

WHAT RUSH HOUR
OFTEN IS.

Now arrange the circled letters to
form the surprise answer, as suggested by the above cartoon.

Answer: THE "◯◯◯◯◯◯" OF THE ◯◯◯◯

…

JUMBLE®

Unscramble these four Jumbles,
one letter to each square, to form
four ordinary words.

UTOOD

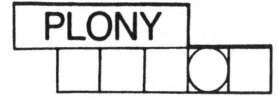

PLONY

RAUBIL

THIGEY

WHAT THEY
CALLED THAT
PIRATE SHIP.

Now arrange the circled letters to
form the surprise answer, as suggested by the above cartoon.

Answer here: THE "◯◯◯◯◯ ◯◯◯◯◯"

JUMBLE.

Unscramble these four Jumbles, one letter to each square, to form four ordinary words.

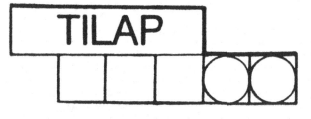

TILAP

SOSYM

NALLEF

HALNIE

Turning pedestrian, eh?

WHERE CAR THIEVES HAVE PUT MANY A MAN.

Now arrange the circled letters to form the surprise answer, as suggested by the above cartoon.

Answer here: "  "

JUMBLE.

Unscramble these four Jumbles,
one letter to each square, to form
four ordinary words.

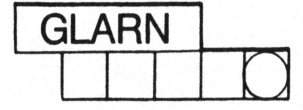

GLARN

UNAFA

DESEEC

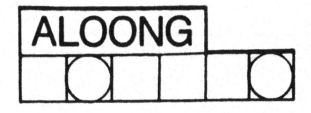

ALOONG

Our first flight
on a supersonic!

Wow! Wait'll
I tell Mabel!

THE ONLY SOUND
THAT TRAVELS
FASTER THAN SOUND.

Now arrange the circled letters to
form the surprise answer, as suggested by the above cartoon.

Print answer here:

JUMBLE.

Unscramble these four Jumbles,
one letter to each square, to form
four ordinary words.

RENID

GALUH

FRUGEE

SERVTY

THEY USED HIM
AS GETAWAY MAN
BECAUSE HE
WAS THIS.

Now arrange the circled letters to
form the surprise answer, as suggested by the above cartoon.

Answer: A " ☐☐☐☐ " ☐☐☐☐☐☐☐

JUMBLE.

Unscramble these four Jumbles, one letter to each square, to form four ordinary words.

RAXOB

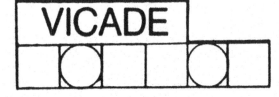

GREME

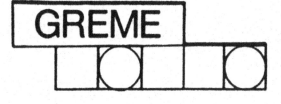

VICADE

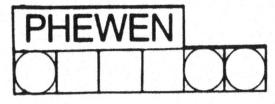

PHEWEN

A NEIGHBOR MIGHT REJOICE AT YOUR GOOD FORTUNE IF IT DOESN'T---

Now arrange the circled letters to form the surprise answer, as suggested by the above cartoon.

Answer here:  HIS

JUMBLE.

Unscramble these four Jumbles,
one letter to each square, to form
four ordinary words.

TALGO

ROBIL

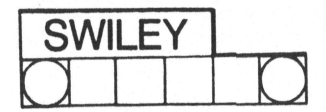

SWILEY

GAHOME

WHAT GREEN IS
FOR A DRIVER.

Now arrange the circled letters to
form the surprise answer, as suggested by the above cartoon.

Answer: THE "⬡⬡⬡⬡⬡" OF ⬡⬡⬡

JUMBLE.

Unscramble these four Jumbles,
one letter to each square, to form
four ordinary words.

TYTIK

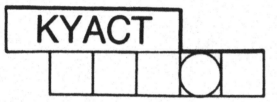

KYACT

FLUDON

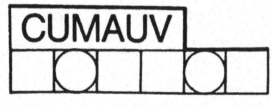

CUMAUV

I think I've lost my wallet

LAST CHANCE Gas

WHAT HE WAS WHEN
HE REALIZED HE HAD
ENOUGH GAS TO
FINISH HIS TRIP.

Now arrange the circled letters to
form the surprise answer, as suggested by the above cartoon.

Print answer here: " ◯◯◯◯◯ – ◯◯◯ "

JUMBLE.

Unscramble these four Jumbles, one letter to each square, to form four ordinary words.

TURET

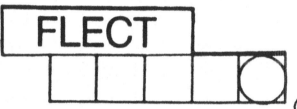

FLECT

REBOFE

NERGEE

AS HE APPROACHED THE RACETRACK, HE SAW THIS SIGN.

Now arrange the circled letters to form the surprise answer, as suggested by the above cartoon.

Answer: " ⭘⭘⭘⭘⭘ FOR ' ⭘⭘⭘⭘⭘⭘⭘ ' "
THE

107

JUMBLE.

Unscramble these four Jumbles,
one letter to each square, to form
four ordinary words.

ZALEH

HAFIT

TIFONY

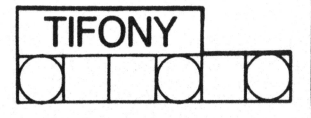

MARROD

TO THE
BIG
CITY

WHAT WAS
DRACULA LOOKING
FOR?

Now arrange the circled letters to
form the surprise answer, as suggested by the above cartoon.

Answer: THE " ⬡⬡⬡⬡ ⬡⬡⬡⬡⬡⬡ "

JUMBLE®

Unscramble these four Jumbles,
one letter to each square, to form
four ordinary words.

LOFUR

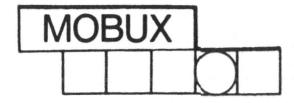

MOBUX

CLUGED

DRIZAL

IF COLUMBUS
WERE ALIVE TODAY,
WHAT WOULD HE BE
BEST KNOWN FOR?

Now arrange the circled letters to
form the surprise answer, as suggested by the above cartoon.

Print answer here:

JUMBLE.

Unscramble these four Jumbles,
one letter to each square, to form
four ordinary words.

EAZUG

FEROC

CUSSID

BENTON

So this is that
lovely place where
you were born

Changed

WHAT NOSTALGIA IS.

Now arrange the circled letters to
form the surprise answer, as suggested by the above cartoon.

Answer: ⬡⬡⬡ WHAT IT ⬡⬡⬡⬡ TO ⬡⬡

JUMBLE.

Unscramble these four Jumbles, one letter to each square, to form four ordinary words.

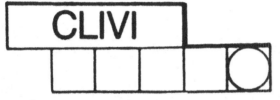

CLIVI

JEGUD

QUILOR

HESTOO

WE CALL A GUY NEUROTIC WHO TELLS US HIS TROUBLES BEFORE WE GET A CHANCE ---

Now arrange the circled letters to form the surprise answer, as suggested by the above cartoon.

Answer here: TO  HIM

JUMBLE.

Unscramble these four Jumbles, one letter to each square, to form four ordinary words.

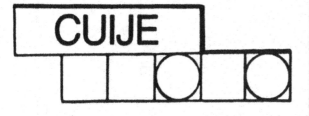

CUIJE

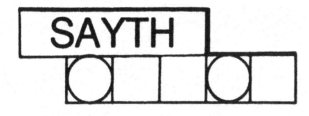

SAYTH

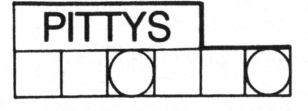

PITTYS

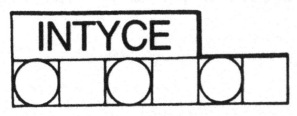

INTYCE

WHAT THEY EXPECTED THE BALL-PLAYER TO DO WHEN HE JOINED THEIR CAMPING PARTY.

Now arrange the circled letters to form the surprise answer, as suggested by the above cartoon.

Answer: "○○○○○○" THE  ○○○○

JUMBLE.

Unscramble these four Jumbles,
one letter to each square, to form
four ordinary words.

TAREF

SULLK

CAJALK

BODLIE

DO THEY HAVE
COURTS OF LAW
AT THE NORTH
POLE?

Now arrange the circled letters to
form the surprise answer, as suggested by the above cartoon.

Print answer here: "  "

JUMBLE.

Unscramble these four Jumbles, one letter to each square, to form four ordinary words.

LOCCI

NELIR

WOELLY

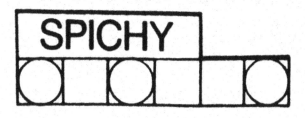

SPICHY

HOW PIZZAS ARE OFTEN DELIVERED.

Now arrange the circled letters to form the surprise answer, as suggested by the above cartoon.

Answer here: BY " ⬡⬡⬡ – ⬡⬡⬡⬡⬡ "

JUMBLE®

Unscramble these four Jumbles, one letter to each square, to form four ordinary words.

ZUZYF

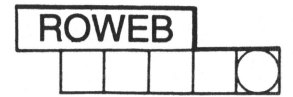

ROWEB

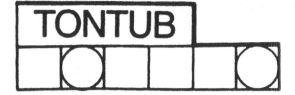

TONTUB

DACAFE

How dare you raise the rates!

WHAT SHE THOUGHT OF THE AIRLINE'S PRICE INCREASE.

Now arrange the circled letters to form the surprise answer, as suggested by the above cartoon.

Print answer here:

JUMBLE®

Unscramble these four Jumbles, one letter to each square, to form four ordinary words.

WREEF

TUISE

LEETEY

DIPALL

We'll have to postpone our trip

WHAT THE SUMMONS FOR JURY DUTY IS CONSIDERED.

Now arrange the circled letters to form the surprise answer, as suggested by the above cartoon.

Answer: THE ⭕⭕⭕⭕⭕ OF THE ⭕⭕⭕

JUMBLE®

Unscramble these four Jumbles,
one letter to each square, to form
four ordinary words.

THRIM

FOREY

RAYPNT

CHOROT

HIS READING OF
SONNETS ON THE
TRAIN WAS KNOWN
AS THIS.

Now arrange the circled letters to
form the surprise answer, as suggested by the above cartoon.

Answer: ⬡⬡⬡⬡⬡ IN ⬡⬡⬡⬡⬡⬡

JUMBLE®

Unscramble these four Jumbles,
one letter to each square, to form
four ordinary words.

NYKAL

REBAG

DINNAL

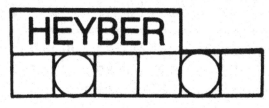

HEYBER

Unfortunately, it was just...

OFTEN THE
EXCUSE FOR A
FENDER BENDER.

Now arrange the circled letters to
form the surprise answer, as suggested by the above cartoon.

Print answer here: A

JUMBLE®

Unscramble these four Jumbles, one letter to each square, to form four ordinary words.

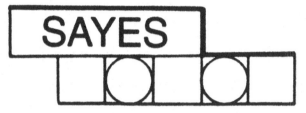

SAYES

CITHY

RAYPER

DILEEY

We'll be landing in a few minutes

WHAT THE LAWYERS CALLED THE FLIGHT UPDATE.

Now arrange the circled letters to form the surprise answer, as suggested by the above cartoon.

Print answer here:

JUMBLE.

Unscramble these four Jumbles,
one letter to each square, to form
four ordinary words.

USAME

CYDER

KLEECH

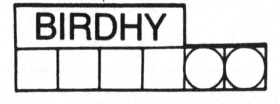

BIRDHY

What are you doing here?

WHAT THE GUARD
DID TO THE
SHIP'S INTRUDER.

Now arrange the circled letters to
form the surprise answer, as suggested by the above cartoon.

Answer here: HE ◯◯◯◯◯◯◯ ◯◯◯

JUMBLE.

Unscramble these four Jumbles, one letter to each square, to form four ordinary words.

STRUB

HOTOT

MOOBBA

TREMIC

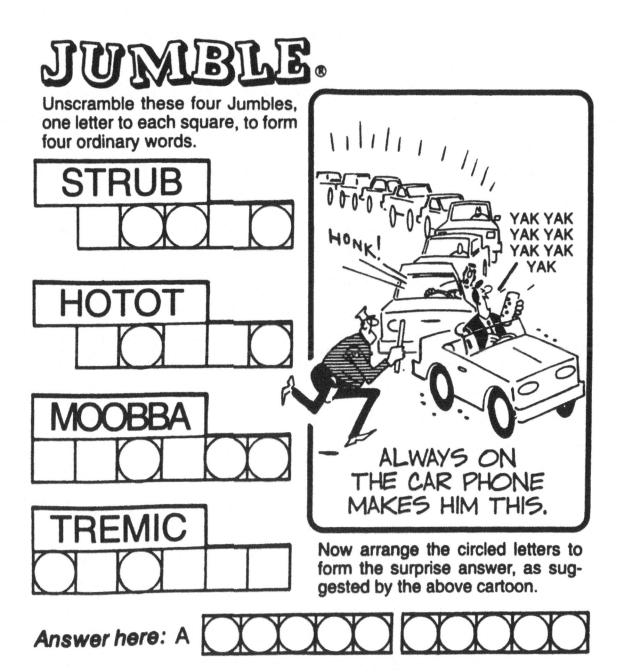

YAK YAK
YAK YAK
YAK YAK
YAK

HONK!

ALWAYS ON THE CAR PHONE MAKES HIM THIS.

Now arrange the circled letters to form the surprise answer, as suggested by the above cartoon.

Answer here: A

JUMBLE®

Unscramble these four Jumbles, one letter to each square, to form four ordinary words.

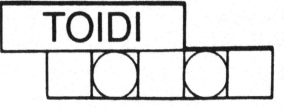

TOIDI

SNAIB

SPOCER

BILBEN

This is a kind of sea animal

HOW THE VISITORS REACTED TO THE SPONGE DIVER'S LECTURE.

Now arrange the circled letters to form the surprise answer, as suggested by the above cartoon.

Answer here: THEY WERE

JUMBLE.

Unscramble these four Jumbles, one letter to each square, to form four ordinary words.

FECAH

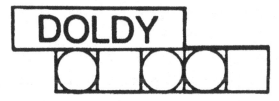
DOLDY

TRAPSY

PORTSY

We need two more lanes

He was a prize student at Oxford

WHAT THE TRANS-PORTATION EXPERT WAS KNOWN AS.

Now arrange the circled letters to form the surprise answer, as suggested by the above cartoon.

Answer: A

JUMBLE.

Unscramble these four Jumbles, one letter to each square, to form four ordinary words.

MARRO

AKELY

NEDDAW

SELIVA

WHAT DRIVERS CALLED THE SLIPPERY ROAD.

Now arrange the circled letters to form the surprise answer, as suggested by the above cartoon.

Print answer here:

JUMBLE®

Unscramble these four Jumbles, one letter to each square, to form four ordinary words.

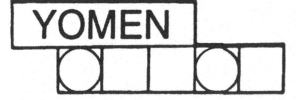

YOMEN

ROBOK

GURTED

ZAHDAR

Nice job

He'll go far

SUCCESSFUL ROAD BUILDERS DO THIS.

Now arrange the circled letters to form the surprise answer, as suggested by the above cartoon.

Answer here:  THE

125

JUMBLE®

Unscramble these four Jumbles, one letter to each square, to form four ordinary words.

ZAWLT

GOLIO

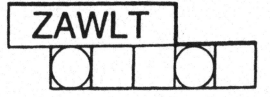

DEGULC

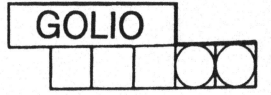

VIQUER

HOW THE ASTRO-NAUTS DESCRIBED THEIR VIEW FROM SPACE.

Now arrange the circled letters to form the surprise answer, as suggested by the above cartoon.

Answer here: ☐☐☐ OF THIS ☐☐☐☐☐

JUMBLE®

Unscramble these four Jumbles, one letter to each square, to form four ordinary words.

MURYM

MUBOX

NOYKED

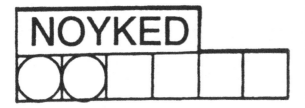

REEBOF

Rate includes meals and lobby show

Another long night

WHAT THE TRAVELER GOT AT THE SMALL-TOWN HOTEL

Now arrange the circled letters to form the surprise answer, as suggested by the above cartoon.

Answer here:  AND

JUMBLE®

Unscramble these four Jumbles, one letter to each square, to form four ordinary words.

DENEY

SATHY

YOSSIF

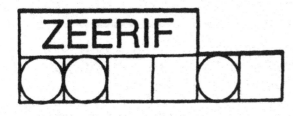

ZEERIF

It's all mine!

WHAT THE NORTH POLE REAL ESTATE TYCOON CONSIDERED HIS HOLDINGS.

Now arrange the circled letters to form the surprise answer, as suggested by the above cartoon.

Answer: HIS

JUMBLE®

Unscramble these four Jumbles, one letter to each square, to form four ordinary words.

CYRUR

TALVE

VAINED

LARCIA

Same work, different day

THE ROAD REPAIRMAN FELT HE WAS THIS.

Now arrange the circled letters to form the surprise answer, as suggested by the above cartoon.

Print answer here:

JUMBLE®

Unscramble these four Jumbles, one letter to each square, to form four ordinary words.

CHULG

OVEBA

DAWPUR

KALCAJ

GET TO WORK!!!

WHAT THE BOSS GAVE THE SLEEPY HOTEL CLERK.

Now arrange the circled letters to form the surprise answer, as suggested by the above cartoon.

Answer here: A

JUMBLE®

Unscramble these four Jumbles,
one letter to each square, to form
four ordinary words.

GOTEB

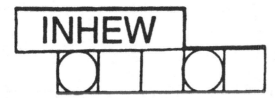

INHEW

GREDLE

NINTTE

Well, we made it. Now what?

WHAT CLIMBERS
ULTIMATELY LOOK
FORWARD TO.

Now arrange the circled letters to
form the surprise answer, as suggested by the above cartoon.

Answer here:

JUMBLE.

Unscramble these four Jumbles, one letter to each square, to form four ordinary words.

MERGI

That's remarkable

It's passed down

ORVAS

SUFOAM

STOLCY

WHERE THE NATIVES' BASKET WEAVING SKILLS CAME FROM.

Now arrange the circled letters to form the surprise answer, as suggested by the above cartoon.

Answer here:

JUMBLE®

Unscramble these four Jumbles, one letter to each square, to form four ordinary words.

GAGBY

HAFFC

DISPUT

YELNOF

More champagne, sir?

Any caviar?

WHAT THE FIRST CLASS TRAVELERS EXPERIENCED.

Now arrange the circled letters to form the surprise answer, as suggested by the above cartoon:

Answer: ⬡⬡⬡⬡⬡⬡⬡ OF ⬡⬡⬡⬡⬡

JUMBLE®

Unscramble these four Jumbles, one letter to each square, to form four ordinary words.

CHABT

GIBLE

DELDUP

BERKAM

This run will show whether you get the job

I hope I make it

HIS BIGGEST FEAR ON THE MOUNTAIN DRIVING TEST.

Now arrange the circled letters to form the surprise answer, as suggested by the above cartoon.

Print answer here: A ⬚⬚⬚ ⬚⬚⬚⬚⬚

JUMBLE®

Unscramble these four Jumbles,
one letter to each square, to form
four ordinary words.

ARCTT

CIRLY

ZEEMYN

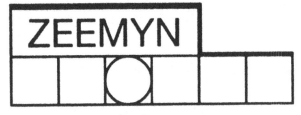

DYRAMI

For the tenth time--
do you know where
you're going?

Uhh...what
was that
address again?

WHERE THE LOST
CAB DRIVER
DROVE HIS FARE.

Now arrange the circled letters to
form the surprise answer, as suggested by the above cartoon.

Print answer here :

JUMBLE®

Unscramble these four Jumbles, one letter to each square, to form four ordinary words.

EGGOR

ILLEB

KRALTE

BLOUFE

That's fifty bucks for the tow

HOW HIS CAR TROUBLE LEFT HIM.

Now arrange the circled letters to form the surprise answer, as suggested by the above cartoon.

Print answer here : " ⬡⬡⬡⬡ " ⬡⬡⬡⬡⬡

JUMBLE®

Unscramble these four Jumbles,
one letter to each square, to form
four ordinary words.

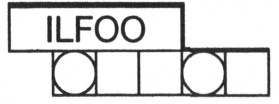

ILFOO

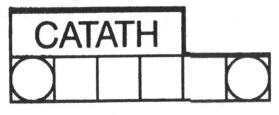

UNESE

CATATH

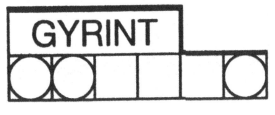

GYRINT

An hour
to go

WHAT THE TRANS-
MISSION MECHANICS
WORKED ON
EVERY DAY.

Now arrange the circled letters to
form the surprise answer, as suggested by the above cartoon.

Print answer here : A

137

JUMBLE®

Unscramble these four Jumbles,
one letter to each square, to form
four ordinary words.

SOIVR

MERRA

ASCUBA

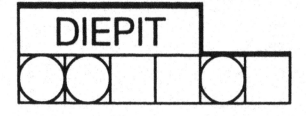

DIEPIT

We're tenth in line
for landing, folks

There goes
my meeting!

A LATE FLIGHT
CAN CAUSE THIS
TO BUILD UP.

Now arrange the circled letters to
form the surprise answer, as suggested by the above cartoon.

Answer here :

JUMBLE®

Unscramble these four Jumbles,
one letter to each square, to form
four ordinary words.

NOPLY

YANON

TUCSOC

RUGLAF

Here's the
down payment

Sign
here

WHAT A NEW
OWNER DOES
BEFORE HE
SAILS HIS BOAT.

Now arrange the circled letters to
form the surprise answer, as suggested by the above cartoon.

Answer here :  A

JUMBLE®

Unscramble these four Jumbles,
one letter to each square, to form
four ordinary words.

RESEA

WYSEN

SATTLE

DAHBEE

You pass

That was
a snap

WHERE THE
SIMPLE DRIVING
TEST PUT HER.

Now arrange the circled letters to
form the surprise answer, as suggested by the above cartoon.

Answer: ON " ⬡⬡⬡⬡⬡ " ⬡⬡⬡⬡⬡⬡⬡

JUMBLE®

Unscramble these four Jumbles,
one letter to each square, to form
four ordinary words.

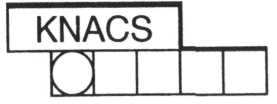

KNACS

KAYLB

UNJAYT

WABUSY

I can't wait to see
the new styles

I'm getting a
lot of toys

MALL

Me, too

HIGHWAYS
LEAD HERE.

Now arrange the circled letters to
form the surprise answer, as suggested by the above cartoon.

Print answer here : THE " ⬡⬡⬡ " ⬡⬡⬡⬡

JUMBLE®

Unscramble these four Jumbles,
one letter to each square, to form
four ordinary words.

VILEA

ROPIR

LAFBLE

INNEAC

That area needs
more elevation

Whew --
almost done

WHEN THE GEOG-
RAPHER FINISHED
HIS MAP, IT WAS----

Now arrange the circled letters to
form the surprise answer, as suggested by the above cartoon.

Print answer here : A

JUMBLE®

Unscramble these four Jumbles,
one letter to each square, to form
four ordinary words.

SABOS

ROCCU

ZARLID

NOOSAL

7-14

WHERE THE
MOTORISTS ALWAYS
GET MAD.

Now arrange the circled letters to
form the surprise answer, as suggested by the above cartoon.

Answer: AT THE " ⃝⃝⃝⃝⃝ " ⃝⃝⃝⃝⃝

JUMBLE®

Unscramble these four Jumbles,
one letter to each square, to form
four ordinary words.

PUROG

RAWLD

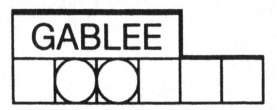

GABLEE

DARAMA

No cars until
this dries

P.D.

WHAT HIGHWAY LANE
STRIPERS DO.

Now arrange the circled letters to
form the surprise answer, as suggested by the above cartoon.

Print answer here : ⬡⬡⬡⬡ THE ⬡⬡⬡⬡

JUMBLE®

Unscramble these four Jumbles, one letter to each square, to form four ordinary words.

LEHEW

INGOR

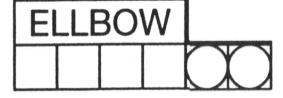

ELLBOW

GORFTO

C'mon, I'm in a hurry

Get in that line

WHAT THE OBNOXIOUS MOTORIST WAS TOLD.

Now arrange the circled letters to form the surprise answer, as suggested by the above cartoon.

Print answer here :

JUMBLE®

Unscramble these four Jumbles,
one letter to each square, to form
four ordinary words.

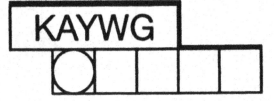

KAYWG

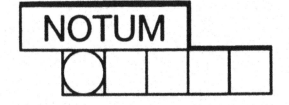

NOTUM

TEENIC

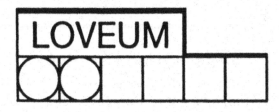

LOVEUM

We'll miss you

CHANGING ADDRESSES
CREATES THIS KIND
OF EXPERIENCE.

Now arrange the circled letters to
form the surprise answer, as suggested by the above cartoon.

Print answer here : "  "

JUMBLE®

Unscramble these four Jumbles,
one letter to each square, to form
four ordinary words.

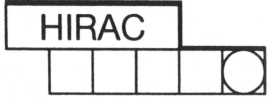

HIRAC

INYAR

BAHFLE

NOPETT

It's
for
you,
George

Take a
message

WHY THE
FISHERMAN DIDN'T
TAKE THE CALL.

Now arrange the circled letters to
form the surprise answer, as suggested by the above cartoon.

Answer here : HE WAS
ON THE ⬡⬡⬡⬡⬡⬡ ⬡⬡⬡⬡

JUMBLE®

Unscramble these four Jumbles,
one letter to each square, to form
four ordinary words.

REWFE

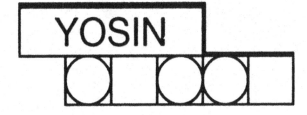

YOSIN

BLIMEN

BORTED

He's waiting for the
crowd to thin out

A GOOD PLACE
TO DO SOME
READING.

Now arrange the circled letters to
form the surprise answer, as suggested by the above cartoon.

Answer: ⬡⬡⬡⬡⬡⬡⬡ THE ⬡⬡⬡⬡⬡

JUMBLE®

Unscramble these four Jumbles,
one letter to each square, to form
four ordinary words.

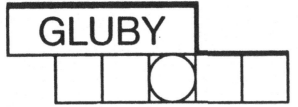

GLUBY

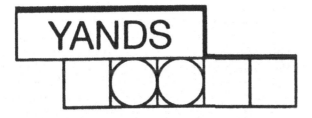

YANDS

GHARNA

INZAIN

Forty minutes
behind schedule

Third time
this week

HOW THE LATE
TRAINS LEFT THE
COMMUTERS.

Now arrange the circled letters to
form the surprise answer, as suggested by the above cartoon.

Print answer here : "  "

JUMBLE®

Unscramble these four Jumbles,
one letter to each square, to form
four ordinary words.

DAUTI

MYPUB

RACLAN

KLUSCE

Runway straight ahead

Flaps

Check

Landing gear

Down

HOW PILOTS AVOID MISTAKES.

Now arrange the circled letters to
form the surprise answer, as suggested by the above cartoon.

Answer: WITH "  "

JUMBLE®

Unscramble these four Jumbles,
one letter to each square, to form
four ordinary words.

TRIHM

GILTH

SNULES

HAXLEE

This is great! That's why it's so popular

WHAT THE
DEMOLITION DERBY
BECAME.

Now arrange the circled letters to
form the surprise answer, as suggested by the above cartoon.

Print answer here : A

JUMBLE®

Unscramble these four Jumbles,
one letter to each square, to form
four ordinary words.

KARCC

RYCED

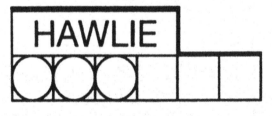

HAWLIE

ETTIPE

Another rejection

WHAT THE CAB
DRIVER TURNED
NOVELIST BECAME.

Now arrange the circled letters to
form the surprise answer, as suggested by the above cartoon.

Answer: A "⬡⬡⬡⬡" ⬡⬡⬡⬡⬡⬡

JUMBLE®

Unscramble these four Jumbles,
one letter to each square, to form
four ordinary words.

LUSKK

NULCE

ACTUFE

ENPLYT

...that old gang of mine...

mi-
mi-
mi-
mi-

WHAT THE SING-
ING MECHANICS
LIKED TO DO.

Now arrange the circled letters to
form the surprise answer, as suggested by the above cartoon.

 *Print answer here :*

JUMBLE®

Unscramble these four Jumbles,
one letter to each square, to form
four ordinary words.

SHOCA

HORAC

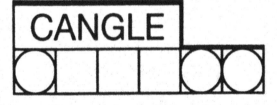

CANGLE

GRUIFE

That'll be $25

Here's my
credit card

THE RESULT OF
STARTING THE
STALLED CAR.

Now arrange the circled letters to
form the surprise answer, as suggested by the above cartoon.

Answer: A

JUMBLE®

Unscramble these four Jumbles,
one letter to each square, to form
four ordinary words.

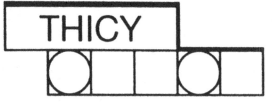

THICY

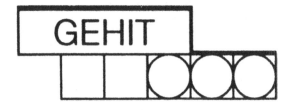

GEHIT

WARMOR

TAIREW

Where is it?

This has a lot of calories, but who cares?

BUS STOP

WHAT SHE
CONSIDERED HER
BUS STOP SNACK.

Now arrange the circled letters to
form the surprise answer, as suggested by the above cartoon.

Answer :  THE

JUMBLE®

Unscramble these four Jumbles,
one letter to each square, to form
four ordinary words.

NAYDD

BUMIE

RAFIAS

SENNIG

My plane
is late

I got
the deal!

THESE ARE
HANDY TO KEEP
YOU IN TOUCH.

Now arrange the circled letters to
form the surprise answer, as suggested by the above cartoon.

Print answer here :

JUMBLE®

Unscramble these four Jumbles,
one letter to each square, to form
four ordinary words.

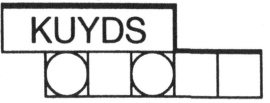

KUYDS

CIKHT

BADCUT

LEKECH

I'll never get to play
with that mob

The dealer won again—
it must be fixed

WHAT THE
GAMBLERS DID ON
THE CROWDED
CASINO BOAT.

Now arrange the circled letters to
form the surprise answer, as suggested by the above cartoon.

Answer : ☐◯◯◯◯◯◯ THE ☐◯◯◯

JUMBLE®

Unscramble these four Jumbles,
one letter to each square, to form
four ordinary words.

AMMIX

SCABI

GLANET

YARREP

Comes with a lot
of accessories

CREDIT DEP'T

$75,000

GOES ALONG
WITH A NEW
CONVERTIBLE.

Now arrange the circled letters to
form the surprise answer, as suggested by the above cartoon.

Print answer here :

JUMBLE®

Unscramble these four Jumbles,
one letter to each square, to form
four ordinary words.

EBBIR

KNITH

DIBRYH

RENACK

I'll let you go this time

SCREECH!

A COP CAN
GIVE THIS TO
A SPEEDING
MOTORIST.

Now arrange the circled letters to
form the surprise answer, as suggested by the above cartoon.

Print answer here : A "  "

JUMBLE.

Unscramble these four Jumbles,
one letter to each square, to form
four ordinary words.

CHITH

TOAFO

SAMTIG

EOPING

Maybe they can tell us
where we are

SPOTTING A TENT
MEANT THIS TO
THE LOST HIKERS.

Now arrange the circled letters to
form the surprise answer, as suggested by the above cartoon.

Print answer here : A

JUMBLE®

Unscramble these four Jumbles,
one letter to each square, to form
four ordinary words.

POEMT

LIWLT

ENMECT

LATOPS

Now I'm
not hungry

THE STORM DID
THIS TO THE
PICNICKERS.

Now arrange the circled letters to
form the surprise answer, as suggested by the above cartoon.

Answer: ☐☐☐ THEIR ☐☐☐☐☐☐☐☐☐

161

JUMBLE.

Unscramble these four Jumbles,
one letter to each square, to form
four ordinary words.

NOKTE

LIMYK

RATYGE

DELBEH

Go ahead, men—
I'll catch up

WHAT THE
TIRED LEADER
WANTED HIS
SCOUTS TO DO.

Now arrange the circled letters to
form the surprise answer, as suggested by the above cartoon.

Print answer here :  A

JUMBLE®

Unscramble these six Jumbles,
one letter to each square,
to form six ordinary words.

TIFELL

LUZZEG

METIKS

JELIGG

DINNAL

NERBAN

Uh oh!

BUMP!

WHAT THE CAPTAIN
HAD WHEN HE SAW
THE ICEBERG.

Now arrange the circled letters
to form the surprise answer, as
suggested by the above cartoon.

Print the
ANSWER here A

JUMBLE®

Unscramble these six Jumbles, one letter to each square, to form six ordinary words.

DICHOR

ELDAHN

PRYSAT

BENRAY

WREABE

CHUGAT

MT. EVEREST SUMMIT

This ought to do it!

WHAT SOME PEOPLE GO TO GREAT LENGTHS TO DO.

Now arrange the circled letters to form the surprise answer, as suggested by the above cartoon.

ANSWER here

THEIR

165

JUMBLE®

Unscramble these six Jumbles, one letter to each square, to form six ordinary words.

GILOOG

SPEBIC

INKELT

OOLANG

SEWNAR

RECHIP

WHAT THEY MIGHT SPEAK IN LONDON'S TRAFALGAR SQUARE.

Now arrange the circled letters to form the surprise answer, as suggested by the above cartoon.

Print the SURPRISE ANSWER here

JUMBLE®

Unscramble these six Jumbles,
one letter to each square,
to form six ordinary words.

AROTTE

OOTARR

TANNIE

BLAVER

SERJEY

KRODEF

Boy—that
takes brains!

IT'S RESPONSIBLE FOR
MUCH PROGRESS IN
THIS COUNTRY.

Now arrange the circled letters
to form the surprise answer, as
suggested by the above cartoon.

Print the SURPRISE
ANSWER here   **THE** ⃝⃝⃝⃝⃝⃝ ⃝⃝⃝⃝⃝

JUMBLE®

Unscramble these six Jumbles,
one letter to each square,
to form six ordinary words.

MIRSUQ

GIXNIF

NAHMLY

EXVONC

BAYTER

SPLEET

WHY IS TODAY'S
WORLD LIKE AN
INCOMPLETE
JIGSAW PUZZLE?

Now arrange the circled letters
to form the surprise answer, as
suggested by the above cartoon.

A ◯◯◯◯◯ IS ◯◯◯◯◯◯◯◯

JUMBLE®

Unscramble these six Jumbles,
one letter to each square,
to form six ordinary words.

MIRNIF

LAPPOR

PIMNED

YERSEG

MOUVLE

ELCHEK

WHAT YOU MIGHT
THINK OF WHEN YOU
SEE A SAILOR WHO
NEEDS A HAIRCUT.

Now arrange the circled letters
to form the surprise answer, as
suggested by the above cartoon.

Print the SURPRISE
ANSWER here

A " ⬡⬡⬡⬡⬡⬡⬡ " ⬡⬡⬡⬡

JUMBLE®

Unscramble these six Jumbles,
one letter to each square,
to form six ordinary words.

KOJECY

EXFLAN

LAWSUR

SKUTEM

BELMAM

TURGED

Behave
yourselves!

WHAT STEAMROLLERS
HELP US DO.

Now arrange the circled letters
to form the surprise answer, as
suggested by the above cartoon.

Print the SURPRISE ANSWER here

JUMBLE®

Unscramble these six Jumbles,
one letter to each square,
to form six ordinary words.

TANCAV

GWEEDD

LEMOTE

THERTE

YAIRFT

MANNEP

No discount?

YOUR FARE SHOULD
BE REDUCED
IF YOU'RE THIS.

Now arrange the circled letters
to form the surprise answer, as
suggested by the above cartoon.

Print the SURPRISE ANSWER here

JUMBLE®

Unscramble these six Jumbles,
one letter to each square,
to form six ordinary words.

TULNAW

CUBDAT

MAIROH

NATQUI

LAGYAX

ROLARP

He won't pay

Take him in

TAXI

YOU'LL BE CHARGED
AFTER A RIDE IN THIS.

Now arrange the circled letters
to form the surprise answer, as
suggested by the above cartoon.

Print the SURPRISE ANSWER here **A**

JUMBLE®

Unscramble these six Jumbles,
one letter to each square,
to form six ordinary words.

LUFNIX

RALLUP

ENDTOE

CLEBUK

WEGNIT

UNROAD

THIS VESSEL CONTAINS
JUST A LITTLE MORE
THAN FOUR QUARTS.

Now arrange the circled letters
to form the surprise answer, as
suggested by the above cartoon.

Print the SURPRISE ANSWER here A "◯◯◯◯◯-◯-◯◯"

JUMBLE®

Unscramble these six Jumbles, one letter to each square, to form six ordinary words.

HODRIC

KUPHOO

HAVEEB

LICIAT

REMIPE

TRUSEY

DOWN WITH

BAN THE BO

WHAT A TAILGATER IS.

Now arrange the circled letters to form the surprise answer, as suggested by the above cartoon.

PRINT YOUR ANSWER IN THE CIRCLES BELOW

A

JUMBLE.

Unscramble these six Jumbles, one letter to each square, to form six ordinary words.

SIMREY

FRILPE

ARUSSE

ENCHEW

TYRITH

ZANATS

WHAT AN OLDSTER SOMETIMES PREFERS.

Now arrange the circled letters to form the surprise answer, as suggested by the above cartoon.

PRINT YOUR ANSWER IN THE CIRCLES BELOW

A ☐☐☐☐☐☐☐ TO A ☐☐☐☐☐☐

JUMBLE.

Unscramble these six Jumbles, one letter to each square, to form six ordinary words.

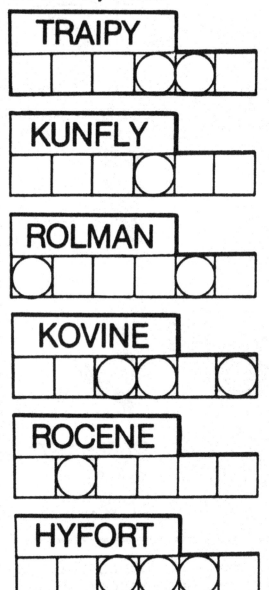

TRAIPY

KUNFLY

ROLMAN

KOVINE

ROCENE

HYFORT

WHAT WOULD YOU SAY IF THE SEA DRIED UP?

Now arrange the circled letters to form the surprise answer, as suggested by the above cartoon.

PRINT YOUR ANSWER IN THE CIRCLES BELOW

"WE ☐☐☐☐☐☐" ☐ A ☐☐☐☐☐☐"

JUMBLE.

Unscramble these six Jumbles, one letter to each square, to form six ordinary words.

TELKIN

DEGAMA

CUPHIC

FRIDAT

GURMOE

SNOOPI

Careful!

WHAT YOU MIGHT END UP WITH IF YOU HAPPEN TO TOUCH POISON IVY WHILE PICKING A FOUR-LEAF CLOVER.

Now arrange the circled letters to form the surprise answer, as suggested by the above cartoon.

PRINT YOUR ANSWER IN THE CIRCLES BELOW

A " ☐☐☐☐ " OF ☐☐☐☐☐ ☐☐☐☐

JUMBLE.

Unscramble these six Jumbles, one letter to each square, to form six ordinary words.

DOLBIE

INGEEN

PHASIM

CLINEP

TURGED

CATCEN

My aching feet!

WHAT THE STRAP-HANGERS' COMPLAINT WAS ONE OF.

Now arrange the circled letters to form the surprise answer, as suggested by the above cartoon.

PRINT YOUR ANSWER IN THE CIRCLES BELOW

" ◯◯◯◯ ◯◯◯◯◯◯◯◯ "

JUMBLE®

Unscramble these six Jumbles, one letter to each square, to form six ordinary words.

GOEMAH

VARQUE

JERIGG

SINOUF

YUGLIT

ENGOUT

You can't throw that out the window

LITTERBUGS FEAR THEM.

Now arrange the circled letters to form the surprise answer, as suggested by the above cartoon.

PRINT YOUR ANSWER IN THE CIRCLES BELOW

JUMBLE®

Unscramble these six Jumbles, one letter to each square, to form six ordinary words.

TOPICE

TOCHEL

MIENER

GOAPAD

SNIPPE

RHAYDL

INN

And don't come back!

INNKEEPERS DO THIS TO DEADBEATS.

Now arrange the circled letters to form the surprise answer, as suggested by the above cartoon.

PRINT YOUR ANSWER IN THE CIRCLES BELOW

○○○ - ○○○○○ ○○○○

JUMBLE®

Unscramble these six Jumbles,
one letter to each square, to form
six ordinary words.

SERVTY

CLARNE

IBBADE

DYKLIN

ODUXTE

YOJECK

F–J   A–E

I was born smack
dab between
both countries

WHAT THE PROBLEM
AT IMMIGRATION
PROVED TO BE.

Now arrange the circled letters to
form the surprise answer, as suggested by the above cartoon.

PRINT YOUR ANSWER IN THE CIRCLES BELOW

A

JUMBLE®

Unscramble these six Jumbles,
one letter to each square, to form
six ordinary words.

CORNEE

LANFEX

THROOC

INGROI

CATNEC

COBUNE

C'mon—
hard eight

Hortense, what
are you
doing here?

WHAT A GAMBLER
LOOKS FORWARD TO.

Now arrange the circled letters to
form the surprise answer, as suggested by the above cartoon.

PRINT YOUR ANSWER IN THE CIRCLES BELOW

A " ⬡⬡⬡⬡⬡⬡ " ⬡⬡⬡⬡⬡⬡⬡⬡⬡

182

JUMBLE®

Unscramble these six Jumbles,
one letter to each square, to form
six ordinary words.

TYRITH

TABLEL

HELSUB

INSPOO

DYGOTS

CLAJEO

10-9-8-7-6

Right
on time

I hope
everything's
A-OK

WHAT THE ASTRO-
NAUT HAD JUST
BEFORE BLAST OFF.

Now arrange the circled letters to
form the surprise answer, as suggested by the above cartoon.

PRINT YOUR ANSWER IN THE CIRCLES BELOW

1. **Jumbles:** HABIT FLOUT BUREAU EMBALM
   Answer: This might be **THERE** in outer space—ETHER

2. **Jumbles:** NATAL ONION JOYFUL STIGMA
   Answer: How an Oriental got to heaven—
   THE ASIAN FLU

3. **Jumbles:** OZONE VITAL IMPEDE POLICY
   Answer: A motive for a journey—A LOCO-MOTIVE

4. **Jumbles:** JEWEL HURRY ORIGIN SYMBOL
   Answer: A cover-up in Indiana—"HOOSIERY"

5. **Jumbles:** ANISE DRAWL CLIENT INCOME
   Answer: What skywriters write—AIRLINES

6. **Jumbles:** FUSSY ROBOT DEVOUR ENTIRE
   Answer: What you might say when you see an intoxicated customs inspector—"SOUSE OF THE BORDER"

7. **Jumbles:** FIERY PAGAN MOBILE IMPAIR
   Answer: Where you might get mail in Ohio—FROM LIMA

8. **Jumbles:** EXILE FRAME ZINNIA AFLOAT
   Answer: What a Moroccan said to someone he hadn't seen in years—YOUR FEZ IS FAMILIAR

9. **Jumbles:** USURP MERGE FLABBY JESTER
   Answer: Currently influential around the southeastern U.S. coast—THE GULF STREAM

10. **Jumbles:** STUNG AGONY HINDER LEEWAY
    Answer: What to say when asked to name the capital of all the states—"WASHINGTON"

11. **Jumbles:** TARRY POKER DEBATE GYRATE
    Answer: Often charged for better service—A BATTERY

12. **Jumbles:** CYNIC GLORY IODINE AMBUSH
    Answer: What the custom inspector said the smuggler's case was—OPEN & SHUT

13. **Jumbles:** CARGO EMPTY AVENUE MYSTIC
    Answer: What they said about the pretty lady cabdriver—YOU "AUTO METER"

14. **Jumbles:** MOLDY ABIDE GUTTER VALISE
    Answer: What they said to the guy who was taking a trip on a tramp steamer—"BUM VOYAGE"

15. **Jumbles:** PUPIL BRAVE MARROW ADVICE
    Answer: This might grow in a junkyard—
    A BUMPER CROP

16. **Jumbles:** SINGE GAUDY PUSHER BEAUTY
    Answer: Small cars relieve this—GAS "PAYIN'S"

17. **Jumbles:** PIVOT FORUM DENTAL DITTO
    Answer: It's the same in many countries—"DITTO"

18. **Jumbles:** PIKER GUEST MISUSE HUNGRY
    Answer: They contract to give you a comfortable ride—
    SPRINGS

19. **Jumbles:** COLIC KINKY UNSAID PLAQUE
    Answer: "Jump, miss"—SKIP

20. **Jumbles:** GUESS MESSY LEGUME POPLAR
    Answer: He declared—he wasn't one!—A SMUGGLER

21. **Jumbles:** MINER SCARF BYWORD DAMPEN
    Answer: May be shot in a boat—RAPIDS

22. **Jumbles:** BERTH NIPPY MAINLY COLUMN
    Answer: **MEN IN PORT** are conspicuous—
    "PROMINENT"

23. **Jumbles:** WHINE CRACK SUNDAE HEARSE
    Answer: How to cut up in a cab—USE A HACKSAW

24. **Jumbles:** ROBIN TULIP SHADOW VOYAGE
    Answer: You wouldn't expect to find her at home!—
    A VISITOR

25. **Jumbles:** RODEO ZOMBI PERSON THWART
    Answer: A traveler has absolutely no chance of getting on this line!—THE HORIZON

26. **Jumbles:** WEARY LOFTY SWERVE INBORN
    Answer: For these opera singers—could be no rest—
    "TENORS"

27. **Jumbles:** PROBE ABATE HAPPEN INSIST
    Answer: Could be the reason—for having married in Spain—"THE SENORA"

28. **Jumbles:** OWING EMERY AMAZON FORBID
    Answer: What you might find in Borneo—on a native—
    "NO ROBE"

29. **Jumbles:** HUMID GLOVE EXOTIC PIGEON
    Answer: What "tequila" is—THE "GULP" OF MEXICO

30. **Jumbles:** TASTY FLUTE WHINNY ORIGIN
    Answer: The train carrying the laundrymen to work was delayed because of this—"WASH OUT" ON THE LINE

31. **Jumbles:** ADULT LINEN PONCHO INFANT
    Answer: What you have to take into consideration these days when you have your tires pumped up—INFLATION

32. **Jumbles:** MANLY ROUSE EXTANT OPIATE
    Answer: What mixing up trains might be for a traveler—
    A "STRAIN"

33. **Jumbles:** PAYEE LINGO HEALTH TEMPER
    Answer: What stories heard during a flight are expected to be—ON A HIGH PLANE

34. **Jumbles:** HOVEL RUSTY LAUNCH OUTCRY
    Answer: The king decided to abdicate rather than risk being this—"THRONE" OUT

35. **Jumbles:** GOOSE ICILY CLOTHE LIZARD
    Answer: What you have to have to spot a glacier—
    GOOD ICE SIGHT

36. **Jumbles:** APPLY SWASH BEFORE INVENT
    Answer: Spots from the rear—"STOPS"

37. **Jumbles:** YODEL AWASH INVITE ORPHAN
    Answer: Our astronauts will land on Mars when they do this—"PLANET" THAT WAY

38. **Jumbles:** SAUTE WHOOP SYSTEM POWDER
    Answer: Why a barefoot kid might remind you of an arctic explorer—
    HE WEARS NO SHOES (wears snowshoes)

39. **Jumbles:** IMPEL NAVAL ZINNIA TRUISM
    Answer: What the musicians said that awful hotel was—
    A "VILE INN" (violin)

40. **Jumbles:** VYING BASIS STUPID INNING
    Answer: What you usually pay when you call on someone—A VISIT

41. **Jumbles:** MOURN BEIGE EMBRYO NEARBY
    Answer: One side of the street usually shows it even—
    NUMBERING

42. **Jumbles:** HIKER DUNCE ARCTIC PARDON
    Answer: In what state are most people born?—
    "THE NUDE"

43. **Jumbles:** FEIGN DRAWL AROUSE BECALM
    Answer: Might be combat pilots in space suits—"ACES"

44. **Jumbles:** ENTRY PANDA DEVOUR HITHER
    Answer: This will help if you're badly tired for driving—
    A RETREAD

45. **Jumbles:** KNIFE SWISH GUITAR FORCED
    Answer: What ice on the road is—SKID STUFF

46. **Jumbles:** SWASH BURST VIABLE COUPLE
    Answer: What a beauty contest judge has to know how to do—PASS ON CURVES

47. **Jumbles:** VITAL MUSIC NINETY FICKLE
    Answer: Why he insisted on wearing seat belts—
    TO SAVE HIS KIN

48. **Jumbles:** NOBLE SHEAF GIGGLE INFECT
Answer: What that frustrated astronaut was always doing at home—BLASTING OFF

49. **Jumbles:** VERVE BELLE TRAGIC AIRWAY
Answer: What they called the man who put glass into the igloo windows—THE "GLACIER"

50. **Jumbles:** SANDY KNELL UPROAR GULLET
Answer: What a backseat driver never seems to do—RUN OUT OF "GAS"

51. **Jumbles:** BUSHY SCARY HANDED EROTIC
Answer: What he apparently took in order to learn to drive—A "CRASH" COURSE

52. **Jumbles:** AWOKE RUMMY CACTUS PICKET
Answer: What the railroad man said to the hobo who was trying to steal a ride—MAKE TRACKS!

53. **Jumbles:** PHOTO SQUAB LEAVEN IMPUGN
Answer: What "HMS Pinafore" could undoubtedly be—"NAME FOR SHIP"

54. **Jumbles:** PAUSE FRAME EXTENT BOTHER
Answer: What was the trouble with the restaurant they opened up on the moon?—IT HAD NO "ATMOSPHERE"

55. **Jumbles:** FLAKE VAGUE AMAZON EMERGE
Answer: Lightly gives you the go-ahead—GREEN

56. **Jumbles:** BEIGE PEONY DISCUS FORGET
Answer: What a murky fog gives drivers—THE "CREEPS"

57. **Jumbles:** EXERT FETCH WALNUT HERALD
Answer: What a rainy day is for a cabdriver—"FARE" WEATHER

58. **Jumbles:** SOOTY OAKEN RATHER MUSTER
Answer: What you might get from astronomers—"NO MORE STARS"

59. **Jumbles:** HUMAN BRASS CUDDLE TEAPOT
Answer: What he was when he saw that tree trunk right in the middle of the road—"STUMPED"

60. **Jumbles:** KNELL FINNY IMPORT GLANCE
Answer: There's usually a fine for parking in any spot that's this—FINE FOR PARKING

61. **Jumbles:** NATAL OUTDO PIGEON TOUCHY
Answer: What form of locomotion is drag racing?—A "LOCO" MOTION

62. **Jumbles:** BIPED IMBUE TUXEDO MANAGE
Answer: What to do when you have the feeling you want to spend more than you can afford—NIP IT IN THE "BUD-GET"

63. **Jumbles:** MOSSY QUEUE MATURE EXODUS
Answer: An impatient driver who has to stop for a traffic light usually does this—"SEES RED"

64. **Jumbles:** BERYL APPLY FILLET MORBID
Answer: The best wine after a long voyage—PORT

65. **Jumbles:** AFTER IMPEL MUFFIN TWINGE
Answer: What a blizzard might do to daily life—"WINTER-UPT IT"

66. **Jumbles:** FRUIT LADLE FACADE JUMPER
Answer: The only time some drivers obey the speed limit is when they're this—IN A TRAFFIC JAM

67. **Jumbles:** TONIC BOGUS TROPHY SMUDGE
Answer: What most vacationers seem to be these days—"MO-TOUR-ISTS"

68. **Jumbles:** BASIC OFTEN REDEEM SUBURB
Answer: What many a used car is not—WHAT IT USED TO BE

69. **Jumbles:** ERUPT YOUNG GUNNER REALTY
Answer: "A man sold me the Nile River for ten dollars."—"E-GYPT YOU" (he gypped you)

70. **Jumbles:** CIVIL FINAL DIVERT JUNGLE
Answer: He wouldn't be in such a hurry if he knew he was this—DRIVING TO JAIL

71. **Jumbles:** LAPEL CREEL TERROR ABRUPT
Answer: What that first tavern in the Arctic was called—THE POLAR BAR

72. **Jumbles:** FEINT ANNOY HIDING EXEMPT
Answer: What bitter cold weather sometimes is—NEXT TO "NOTHING"

73. **Jumbles:** FAUNA HEAVY MEMORY AUTUMN
Answer: Pollution is the contamination of nature by this—HUMAN NATURE

74. **Jumbles:** TROTH ENTRY JAGUAR REBUKE
Answer: What the story about the onion crop was—A TEARJERKER

75. **Jumbles:** YODEL CAPON ZEALOT JUMPER
Answer: That reckless chauffeur must have had a license to drive—PEOPLE CRAZY

76. **Jumbles:** EATEN ARDOR DECENT PHYSIC
Answer: A driver is a guy who forgets that he used to be this—A PEDESTRIAN

77. **Jumbles:** SOGGY HAVOC TARGET INVEST
Answer: A pedestrian is a person who has learned that is doesn't always pay to—GO STRAIGHT

78. **Jumbles:** MOGUL PIVOT DECADE REALTY
Answer: If you're lucky, that used car will be a pleasure to ride; if not,—TO "DERIDE"

79. **Jumbles:** BARGE AISLE DRAGON PESTLE
Answer: What a person who has failed to keep up his payments on the car is called—A PEDESTRIAN

80. **Jumbles:** OBESE USURY FLIMSY BUSILY
Answer: The only sure way of catching the next train is to—MISS THE ONE BEFORE

81. **Jumbles:** ODIUM ANKLE BYGONE DIGEST
Answer: How spring often comes—"SODDEN-LY"

82. **Jumbles:** PRUNE FETID STICKY EXPOSE
Answer: What a smuggler doesn't have—A SENSE OF DUTY

83. **Jumbles:** CAMEO FATAL DARING BOILED
Answer: What a parent's major problem sometimes is—A MINOR

84. **Jumbles:** FUDGE AGILE BUCKLE CRAYON
Answer: What happens when automobiles are so close together they can't move?—GRIDLOCK

85. **Jumbles:** SHEEP EXACT MARROW TAWDRY
Answer: If you lend a pretended "friend" money, and never see him again—IT WAS WORTH IT

86. **Jumbles:** GUARD BRAND RAMROD UNEASY
Answer: That pioneer blazed a trail through the wilderness, but now his descendants—BURN UP THE ROAD

87. **Jumbles:** AWARD MOUSE HAGGLE VERIFY
Answer: That road hog was willing to meet any other driver—MORE THAN HALFWAY

88. **Jumbles:** RODEO AGENT DRIVEL WOEFUL
Answer: What a revolution makes—THE WORLD GO ROUND

89. **Jumbles:** BIRCH ICING CORRAL KNIGHT
Answer: All the crooks in that polluted city seem to have vanished—INTO THICK AIR

90. **Jumbles:** EIGHT LIMIT HEAVEN ADRIFT
Answer: The best way to stop the noise in the back of your car—LET HIM DRIVE

91. **Jumbles:** KHAKI ADULT JITNEY MYSTIC
Answer: When a group of friends began playing cards on the plane, they agreed that—THE SKY WAS THE LIMIT

92. **Jumbles:** TARDY BASIN NEARBY EMPIRE
Answer: Might describe the planet Mars—"RED—BARREN"

93. **Jumbles:** PURGE BARGE HINDER VORTEX
Answer: Astronomy might be this—OVER ONE'S HEAD

94. **Jumbles:** BUILT RAPID DELUXE PUMICE
Answer: A paratrooper is just about the only person who can climb down a tree—HE NEVER CLIMBED UP

95. **Jumbles:** CEASE DOUBT CRAFTY SEPTIC
Answer: When he stayed too long, the guest became this—A PEST

96. **Jumbles:** RAINY EMBER REDUCE TAUGHT
Answer: She always drives very slowly because she wants to do anything—TO STAY UNDER THIRTY

97. **Jumbles:** CROWN BRAWL PLEDGE ALIGHT
Answer: What rush hour often is—THE "CRAWL" OF THE WILD

98. **Jumbles:** OUTDO PYLON BURIAL EIGHTY
Answer: What they called that pirate ship—THE "THUG BOAT"

99. **Jumbles:** PLAIT MOSSY FALLEN INHALE
Answer: Where car thieves have put many a man—"ON HIS FEET"

100. **Jumbles:** GNARL FAUNA SECEDE LAGOON
Answer: The only sound that travels faster than sound—SCANDAL

101. **Jumbles:** DINER LAUGH REFUGE VESTRY
Answer: They used him as getaway man because he was this—A "SAFE" DRIVER

102. **Jumbles:** BORAX MERGE ADVICE NEPHEW
Answer: A neighbor might rejoice at your good fortune if it doesn't—EXCEED HIS OWN

103. **Jumbles:** GLOAT BROIL WISELY HOMAGE
Answer: What green is for a driver—THE "LIGHT" OF WAY

104. **Jumbles:** KITTY TACKY UNFOLD VACUUM
Answer: What he was when he realized he had enough gas to finish his trip—"TANK-FUL"

105. **Jumbles:** UTTER CLEFT BEFORE RENEGE
Answer: As he approached the racetrack, he saw this sign—TURN FOR THE "BETTOR"

106. **Jumbles:** HAZEL FAITH NOTIFY RAMROD
Answer: What was Dracula looking for?—THE "MAIN ARTERY"

107. **Jumbles:** FLOUR BUXOM CUDGEL LIZARD
Answer: If Columbus were alive today, what would he be best known for?—OLD AGE

108. **Jumbles:** GAUZE FORCE DISCUS BONNET
Answer: What nostalgia is—NOT WHAT IT USED TO BE

109. **Jumbles:** CIVIL JUDGE LIQUOR SOOTHE
Answer: We call a guy neurotic who tells us his troubles before we get a chance—TO TELL HIM OURS

110. **Jumbles:** JUICE HASTY TYPIST NICETY
Answer: What they expected the ballplayer to do when he joined their camping party—"PITCH" THE TENT

111. **Jumbles:** AFTER SKULL JACKAL BOILED
Answer: Do they have courts of law at the North Pole?—"JUST ICE" (justice)

112. **Jumbles:** COLIC LINER YELLOW PHYSIC
Answer: How pizzas are often delivered—BY "PIE-CYCLE"

113. **Jumbles:** FUZZY BOWER BUTTON FACADE
Answer: What she thought of the airline's price increase—UN-FARE!

114. **Jumbles:** FEWER SUITE EYELET PALLID
Answer: What the summons for jury duty is considered—THE LETTER OF THE LAW

115. **Jumbles:** MIRTH FOYER PANTRY COHORT
Answer: His reading of sonnets on the train was known as this—POETRY IN MOTION

116. **Jumbles:** LANKY BARGE INLAND HEREBY
Answer: Often the excuse for a fender bender—A BAD BRAKE

117. **Jumbles:** ESSAY ITCHY PRAYER EYELID
Answer: What the lawyers called the flight update—"HERE" SAY

118. **Jumbles:** AMUSE DECRY HECKLE HYBRID
Answer: What the guard did to the ship's intruder—HE DECKED HIM

119. **Jumbles:** BURST TOOTH BAMBOO METRIC
Answer: Always on the car phone makes him this—A MOTOR MOUTH

120. **Jumbles:** IDIOT BASIN CORPSE NIBBLE
Answer: How the visitors reacted to the sponge diver's lecture—THEY WERE ABSORBED

121. **Jumbles:** CHAFE ODDLY PASTRY SPORTY
Answer: What the transportation expert was known as—A ROADS SCHOLAR

122. **Jumbles:** ARMOR LEAKY DAWNED VALISE
Answer: What drivers called the slippery road—SKID ROW

123. **Jumbles:** MONEY BROOK TRUDGE HAZARD
Answer: Successful road builders do this—MAKE THE GRADE

124. **Jumbles:** WALTZ IGLOO CUDGEL QUIVER
Answer: How the astronauts described their view from space—OUT OF THIS WORLD

125. **Jumbles:** RUMMY BUXOM DONKEY BEFORE
Answer: What the traveler got at the small-town hotel—ROOM AND BORED

126. **Jumbles:** NEEDY HASTY OSSIFY FRIEZE
Answer: What the North Pole real estate tycoon considered his holdings—HIS FROZEN ASSETS

127. **Jumbles:** CURRY VALET INVADE RACIAL
Answer: The road repairman felt he was this—IN A RUT

128. **Jumbles:** GULCH ABOVE UPWARD JACKAL
Answer: What the boss gave the sleepy hotel clerk—A WAKEUP CALL

129. **Jumbles:** BEGOT WHINE LEDGER INTENT
Answer: What climbers ultimately look forward to—GETTING DOWN

130. **Jumbles:** GRIME SAVOR FAMOUS COSTLY
Answer: Where the natives' basket weaving skills came from—GRASS ROOTS

131. **Jumbles:** BAGGY CHAFF STUPID FELONY
Answer: What the first class travelers experienced—FLIGHTS OF FANCY

132. **Jumbles:** BATCH BILGE PUDDLE EMBARK
Answer: His biggest fear on the mountain driving test—A BAD GRADE

133. **Jumbles:** TRACT LYRIC ENZYME MYRIAD
Answer: Where the lost cab driver drove his fare—CRAZY

134. **Jumbles:** GORGE LIBEL TALKER BEFOUL
Answer: How his car trouble left him—"FLAT" BROKE

135. **Jumbles:** FOLIO ENSUE ATTACH TRYING
Answer: What the transmission mechanics worked on every day—A GEAR SHIFT

136. **Jumbles:** VISOR REARM ABACUS PITIED
Answer: A late flight can cause this to build up—AIR PRESSURE

137. **Jumbles:** PYLON ANNOY STUCCO FRUGAL
Answer: What a new owner does before he sails his boat—FLOATS A LOAN

138. **Jumbles:** ERASE NEWSY LATEST BEHEAD
Answer: Where the simple driving test put her—ON "EASY" STREET

139. **Jumbles:** SNACK BALKY JAUNTY SUBWAY
Answer: Highways lead here—THE "BUY" WAYS

140. **Jumbles:** ALIVE PRIOR BEFALL CANINE
Answer: When the geographer finished his map it was—A RELIEF

141. **Jumbles:** BASSO OCCUR LIZARD SALOON
Answer: Where the motorists always get mad—AT THE "CROSS" ROADS

142. **Jumbles:** GROUP DRAWL BEAGLE ARMADA
Answer: What highway lane stripers do—
RULE THE ROAD

143. **Jumbles:** WHEEL GROIN BELLOW FORGOT
Answer: What the obnoxious motorist was told—
WHERE TO GO

144. **Jumbles:** GAWKY MOUNT ENTICE VOLUME
Answer: Changing addresses creates this kind of experience—"MOVING"

145. **Jumbles:** CHAIR RAINY BEHALF POTENT
Answer: Why the fisherman didn't take the call—
HE WAS ON THE OTHER LINE

146. **Jumbles:** FEWER NOISY NIMBLE DEBTOR
Answer: A good place to do some reading—
BETWEEN THE LINES

147. **Jumbles:** BULGY SANDY HANGAR ZINNIA
Answer: How the late trains left the commuters—
"RAILING"

148. **Jumbles:** AUDIT BUMPY CARNAL SUCKLE
Answer: How pilots avoid mistakes—
WITH "PLANE" TALK

149. **Jumbles:** MIRTH LIGHT UNLESS EXHALE
Answer: What the demolition derby became—
A SMASH HIT

150. **Jumbles:** CRACK DECRY AWHILE PETITE
Answer: What the cab driver turned novelist became—
A "HACK" WRITER

151. **Jumbles:** SKULK UNCLE FAUCET PLENTY
Answer: What the singing mechanics liked to do—
TUNE UPS

152. **Jumbles:** CHAOS ROACH GLANCE FIGURE
Answer: The result of starting the stalled car—
A CHARGE CHARGE

153. **Jumbles:** ITCHY EIGHT MARROW WAITER
Answer: What she considered her bus stop snack—
WORTH THE WEIGHT

154. **Jumbles:** DANDY IMBUE SAFARI ENSIGN
Answer: These are handy to keep you in touch—
FINGERS

155. **Jumbles:** DUSKY THICK ABDUCT HECKLE
Answer: What the gamblers did on the crowded casino boat—STACKED THE DECK

156. **Jumbles:** MAXIM BASIC TANGLE PRAYER
Answer: Goes along with a new convertible—
PAYMENTS

157. **Jumbles:** BRIBE THINK HYBRID CANKER
Answer: A cop can give this to a speeding motorist—
A "BRAKE"

158. **Jumbles:** HITCH AFOOT STIGMA PIGEON
Answer: Spotting a tent meant this to the lost hikers—
A CAMP SIGHT

159. **Jumbles:** TEMPO TWILL CEMENT POSTAL
Answer: The storm did this to the picnickers—
WET THEIR APPETITES

160. **Jumbles:** TOKEN MILKY GYRATE BEHELD
Answer: What the tired leader wanted his scouts to do—
TAKE A HIKE

161. **Jumbles:** FILLET GUZZLE KISMET JIGGLE INLAND BANNER
Answer: What the captain had when he saw the iceberg—A SINKING FEELING

162. **Jumbles:** ORCHID HANDLE PASTRY NEARBY BEWARE CAUGHT
Answer: What some people go to great lengths to do—
CHANGE THEIR WIDTHS

163. **Jumbles:** GIGOLO BICEPS TINKLE LAGOON ANSWER CIPHER
Answer: What they might speak in London's Trafalgar Square—PIGEON ENGLISH

164. **Jumbles:** ROTATE ORATOR INNATE VERBAL JERSEY FORKED
Answer: It's responsible for much progress in this country—THE YANKEE NOODLE

165. **Jumbles:** SQUIRM FIXING HYMNAL CONVEX BETRAY PESTLE
Why is today's world like an incomplete jigsaw puzzle?
A PEACE IS MISSING

166. **Jumbles:** INFIRM POPLAR IMPEND GEYSER VOLUME HECKLE
Answer: What you might think of when you see a sailor who needs a haircut—A "CLIPPER" SHIP

167. **Jumbles:** JOCKEY FLAXEN WALRUS MUSKET EMBALM TRUDGE
Answer: What steamrollers help us do—MEND OUR WAYS

168. **Jumbles:** VACANT WEDGED OMELET TETHER RATIFY PENMAN
Your fare should be reduced if you're this—
OVERWEIGHT

169. **Jumbles:** WALNUT ABDUCT MOHAIR QUAINT GALAXY PARLOR
You'll be charged after a ride in this—A PATROL WAGON

170. **Jumbles:** INFLUX PLURAL DENOTE BUCKLE TWINGE AROUND
This vessel contains just a little more than four quarts—A "GALL-E-ON"

171. **Jumbles:** ORCHID HOOKUP BEHAVE ITALIC EMPIRE SURETY
What a tailgater is—A BUMPER STICKER

172. **Jumbles:** MISERY PILFER ASSURE WHENCE THIRTY STANZA
Answer: What an oldster sometimes prefers—
A SIESTA TO A FIESTA

173. **Jumbles:** PARITY FLUNKY NORMAL INVOKE ENCORE FROTHY
Answer: "What would you say if the sea dried up?"—
"WE HAVEN'T A NOTION"

174. **Jumbles:** TINKLE DAMAGE HICCUP ADRIFT MORGUE POISON
Answer: What you might end up with if you happen to touch poison ivy while picking a four-leaf clover—
A "RASH" OF GOOD LUCK

175. **Jumbles:** BOILED ENGINE MISHAP PENCIL TRUDGE ACCENT
Answer: What the straphangers' complaint was one of—
"LONG STANDING"

176. **Jumbles:** HOMAGE JIGGER GUILTY QUAVER FUSION TONGUE
Answer: Litterbugs fear them—GRIME FIGHTERS

177. **Jumbles:** POETIC ERMINE PEPSIN CLOTHE PAGODA HARDLY
Answer: Innkeepers do this to deadbeats—
DIS-LODGE THEM

178. **Jumbles:** VESTRY BABIED TUXEDO LANCER KINDLY JOCKEY
Answer: What the problem at immigration proved to be—
A BORDERLINE CASE

179. **Jumbles:** ENCORE COHORT ACCENT FLAXEN ORIGIN BOUNCE
Answer: What a gambler looks forward to—
A "CHANCE" ENCOUNTER

180. **Jumbles:** THIRTY BUSHEL STODGY BALLET POISON CAJOLE
Answer: What the astronaut had just before blast off—
SECOND THOUGHTS

Need More Jumbles®?

Order any of these books through your bookseller or call Triumph Books toll-free at 800-335-5323.

Jumble® Books

More than 175 puzzles each!

Cowboy Jumble®
ISBN: 978-1-62937-355-3

Jammin' Jumble®
ISBN: 1-57243-844-4

Java Jumble®
ISBN: 978-1-60078-415-6

Jazzy Jumble®
ISBN: 978-1-57243-962-7

Jet Set Jumble®
ISBN: 978-1-60078-353-1

Joyful Jumble®
ISBN: 978-1-60078-079-0

Juke Joint Jumble®
ISBN: 978-1-60078-295-4

Jumble® Anniversary
ISBN: 987-1-62937-734-6

Jumble® at Work
ISBN: 1-57243-147-4

Jumble® Ballet
ISBN: 978-1-62937-616-5

Jumble® Birthday
ISBN: 978-1-62937-652-3

Jumble® Celebration
ISBN: 978-1-60078-134-6

Jumble® Circus
ISBN: 978-1-60078-739-3

Jumble® Cuisine
ISBN: 978-1-62937-735-3

Jumble® Drag Race
ISBN: 978-1-62937-483-3

Jumble® Ever After
ISBN: 978-1-62937-785-8

Jumble® Explorer
ISBN: 978-1-60078-854-3

Jumble® Explosion
ISBN: 978-1-60078-078-3

Jumble® Fever
ISBN: 1-57243-593-3

Jumble® Fiesta
ISBN: 1-57243-626-3

Jumble® Fun
ISBN: 1-57243-379-5

Jumble® Galaxy
ISBN: 978-1-60078-583-2

Jumble® Garden
ISBN: 978-1-62937-653-0

Jumble® Genius
ISBN: 1-57243-896-7

Jumble® Geography
ISBN: 978-1-62937-615-8

Jumble® Getaway
ISBN: 978-1-60078-547-4

Jumble® Gold
ISBN: 978-1-62937-354-6

Jumble® Grab Bag
ISBN: 1-57243-273-X

Jumble® Gymnastics
ISBN: 978-1-62937-306-5

Jumble® Jackpot
ISBN: 1-57243-897-5

Jumble® Jailbreak
ISBN: 978-1-62937-002-6

Jumble® Jambalaya
ISBN: 978-1-60078-294-7

Jumble® Jamboree
ISBN: 1-57243-696-4

Jumble® Jitterbug
ISBN: 978-1-60078-584-9

Jumble® Journey
ISBN: 978-1-62937-549-6

Jumble® Jubilation
ISBN: 978-1-62937-784-1

Jumble® Jubilee
ISBN: 1-57243-231-4

Jumble® Juggernaut
ISBN: 978-1-60078-026-4

Jumble® Junction
ISBN: 1-57243-380-9

Jumble® Jungle
ISBN: 978-1-57243-961-0

Jumble® Kingdom
ISBN: 978-1-62937-079-8

Jumble® Knockout
ISBN: 978-1-62937-078-1

Jumble® Madness
ISBN: 1-892049-24-4

Jumble® Magic
ISBN: 978-1-60078-795-9

Jumble® Marathon
ISBN: 978-1-60078-944-1

Jumble® Neighbor
ISBN: 978-1-62937-845-9

Jumble® Parachute
ISBN: 978-1-62937-548-9

Jumble® Safari
ISBN: 978-1-60078-675-4

Jumble® See & Search
ISBN: 1-57243-549-6

Jumble® See & Search 2
ISBN: 1-57243-734-0

Jumble® Sensation
ISBN: 978-1-60078-548-1

Jumble® Surprise
ISBN: 1-57243-320-5

Jumble® Symphony
ISBN: 978-1-62937-131-3

Jumble® Theater
ISBN: 978-1-62937-484-03

Jumble® University
ISBN: 978-1-62937-001-9

Jumble® Unleashed
ISBN: 978-1-62937-844-2

Jumble® Vacation
ISBN: 978-1-60078-796-6

Jumble® Wedding
ISBN: 978-1-62937-307-2

Jumble® Workout
ISBN: 978-1-60078-943-4

Jumpin' Jumble®
ISBN: 978-1-60078-027-1

Lunar Jumble®
ISBN: 978-1-60078-853-6

Monster Jumble®
ISBN: 978-1-62937-213-6

Mystic Jumble®
ISBN: 978-1-62937-130-6

Outer Space Jumble®
ISBN: 978-1-60078-416-3

Rainy Day Jumble®
ISBN: 978-1-60078-352-4

Ready, Set, Jumble®
ISBN: 978-1-60078-133-0

Rock 'n' Roll Jumble®
ISBN: 978-1-60078-674-7

Royal Jumble®
ISBN: 978-1-60078-738-6

Sports Jumble®
ISBN: 1-57243-113-X

Summer Fun Jumble®
ISBN: 1-57243-114-8

Touchdown Jumble®
ISBN: 978-1-62937-212-9

Travel Jumble®
ISBN: 1-57243-198-9

TV Jumble®
ISBN: 1-57243-461-9

Oversize Jumble® Books

More than 500 puzzles each!

Generous Jumble®
ISBN: 1-57243-385-X

Giant Jumble®
ISBN: 1-57243-349-3

Gigantic Jumble®
ISBN: 1-57243-426-0

Jumbo Jumble®
ISBN: 1-57243-314-0

The Very Best of Jumble® BrainBusters
ISBN: 1-57243-845-2

Jumble® Crosswords™

More than 175 puzzles each!

More Jumble® Crosswords™
ISBN: 1-57243-386-8

Jumble® Crosswords™ Jackpot
ISBN: 1-57243-615-8

Jumble® Crosswords™ Jamboree
ISBN: 1-57243-787-1

Jumble® BrainBusters™

More than 175 puzzles each!

Jumble® BrainBusters™
ISBN: 1-892049-28-7

Jumble® BrainBusters™ II
ISBN: 1-57243-424-4

Jumble® BrainBusters™ III
ISBN: 1-57243-463-5

Jumble® BrainBusters™ IV
ISBN: 1-57243-489-9

Jumble® BrainBusters™ 5
ISBN: 1-57243-548-8

Jumble® BrainBusters™ Bonanza
ISBN: 1-57243-616-6

Boggle™ BrainBusters™
ISBN: 1-57243-592-5

Boggle™ BrainBusters™ 2
ISBN: 1-57243-788-X

Jumble® BrainBusters™ Junior
ISBN: 1-892049-29-5

Jumble® BrainBusters™ Junior II
ISBN: 1-57243-425-2

Fun in the Sun with Jumble® BrainBusters™
ISBN: 1-57243-733-2